CANNABIS COOKBOOK 2022

DIY Guide for Cannabis Kitchen, Recipes for Brownies, Cakes, snacks & Much More

ELIZABETH FLOURNOY

DISCLAIMER NOTICE

Please note the information contained in this document is for educational and entertainment purposes only. All effort has been executed to present accurate, up-to-date, and reliable, complete information. No warranties of any kind are declared or implied. Readers acknowledge that the author is not engaging in the rendering of legal, financial, medical, or professional before attempting any techniques outlined in this book.

By reading this document, the reader agrees that under no circumstances is the author responsible for any losses, direct or indirect, which are incurred as a result of the use of the information contained in this document, including, but not limited to, - errors, omissions, or inaccuracies

TABLE OF CONTENTS

INTRODUCTION

Dry leaves, flowers, and seeds of marijuana are beneficial to use for different health problems. You can smoke it as a cigarette or pipe. Some people mixed it with food and beverages to improve their health. Smoking cannabis as a joint can help you to enjoy its benefits within a few minutes because you can experience immediate sensation. Its short-term effects may continue for two to three hours, but long-term effects can last longer. Mental consequences of marijuana smoke are severe, but there are a few tips for the use of this herb: Ingestible oils of cannabis are a concentrated form of this herb, and you can use it in capsule form. One can directly consume in food or drink. Powerful effects can induce ingestible oils, but you should take a mindful dose of these oils. Tinctures are infused liquids to extract cannabis compounds, and these are used as an alcohol soak and directly used beneath the tongue. Unlike infused foods and ingestible oils, these tinctures enter the bloodstream and allow fast-acting effects for lots of health benefits. A variety of potencies and flavors are available to cater your specific preferences or therapeutic needs.

Consuming cannabis can be great for those people who are interested in smoking it. To get psychoactive useful of cannabis, you have to heat them in some way be- cause eating this weed straight will not work. In this Cannabis Cookbook, you will get 25 recipes to make Cannabis Cake, desserts, and other recipes. You can enjoy the benefits and great taste of marijuana aka cannabis. Follow these recipes and learn How to Make Cannabis Oil.

CHAPTER 1
CANNA RECIPES

Cannabutter

Ingredients

- 1-ounce cannabis
- ½ pound butter, 2 sticks

How To:

1. Take a stainless steel pan and place it over medium heat
2. Add butter and cannabis and let them melt
3. While heating, fill up the pan about halfway with water and lower down the heat

4. Let the mixture simmer for 30 minutes

5. After 30 minutes, strain the liquids through a fine metal mesh/strainer into a bowl and remove any solid chunks of the cannabis plant

6. Press the solid chunks down to squeeze out any liquid

7. Pass the strained liquid through a cheesecloth to remove any remaining impurities

8. Transfer the double-strained liquid in an airtight container and keep it in your fridge

9. Once the liquid cools and solidifies, the butter will float to the top, which you can skim off any use for any of the recipes in this book

Cannamilk

Ingredients

- ¼ cup finely ground Cannabis Strain

- 5 cups whole milk

How To:

1. Create a double boiler over your stove

2. Bring whole milk to a low boil and let it simmer

3. Add Cannabis into the low boiling milk, making sure to keep stirring it constantly until the plant has dissolved completely

4. Lower down the heat of the double-boiler to low and stir for 30-45 minutes

5. Remove milk from double boiler and strain through a cheesecloth

6. Squeeze as much Cannamilk as possible into a heatproof container

7. Use as needed!

Cannaoil

Ingredients

- 48 ounces Canola oil

- 1-ounce Marijuana, finely ground

How To:

1. Take your oil bottle and pour the oil into a pot

2. Transfer the pot to your stove and place it over medium-low heat

3. Let it heat up and make sure that it doesn't start boiling

4. Add marijuana to the pot

5. Now keep the oil over very low heat and keep stirring it for every 10-20 minutes

6. The process is needed to be done for about 2-3 hours to allow the resin extraction to work properly

7. The key thing to remember is that you should never let the oil reach a boil. Otherwise, the taste will be ruined

8. After 2-3 hours, remove the heat and let the oil cool for 45 minutes

9. Take the pot off and pour oil through a fine metal strainer and into a heatproof container

10. Repeat this process 2-3 times to ensure that there are no unwanted solid bits

11. Use as needed!

Cannabis Tincture (Cold Method)

INGREDIENTS

- 1 ounce cannabis
- 1 pint 95% Ethanol (190 Proof)

DIRECTIONS

You will need 1 ounce of cannabis for every pint of ethanol. Some good spirits to use would be Everclear, 151 Rum, or White Lightning due to the high proof. You want an alcohol with 95% ethanol, or a 190-proof alcohol to obtain the best results. The night before you make this, leave your bud close the jar and shake for 5 minutes, then return to freezer. Continue to agitate the mixture every few hours with refreezing. Continue this process anywhere from 3 days to 9 weeks, however patient you are really. Remember, the longer the better. When you are done with that process, pour the liquid through cheesecloth. You can save the "ball" of cheesecloth for topical use, or run it through a coffee filter. Make sure to squeeze any remaining liquid out. You might want to wear gloves during this process, as the solution might be pretty strong. The color of your final product is dependent on what percent ethanol you used. If you used a 95% ethanol solution, your tincture should be pale green to golden. If you used

151 rum, it should be an amber color. If your tincture is a dark green that means excess plant material is present. This does not affect the potency though; it just means it won't taste very good. It's a good idea to add some flavor extracts, like vanilla or raspberry, to change the taste of your tincture.

NOTES

Making a tincture via the cold method preserves the integrity of cannabinoids. Always use the best quality cannabis for the best results. Your cannabis should be completely dry and mold free.

Cannabis Tincture (Warm Method)

INGREDIENTS

- 1 ounce cannabis, Roughly Chopped
- 1 pint 95% Ethanol (190 Proof)

DIRECTIONS

Place the cannabis and ethanol in a large glass Mason jar. Shake at least once a day. Place the jar in a brown paper bag. Leave in a warm spot, like near the window, for 30-60 days. The mixture should turn a very dark green. Strain with a cheesecloth like in the cold method, making sure to squeeze any excess liquid. This tincture has a nasty taste, but it is very powerful. It may upset fragile stomachs. You should take the tincture orally in cranberry juice or coffee with sugar. Store your tincture in a light-blocking glass jar in a cool, dry place (like the refrigerator or freezer). You can keep the cheesecloth in the freezer as well and apply it over an area of the skin for a few minutes with gentle rubbing.

NOTES

The main difference between this method and the cold method is the preparation of materials. Light must be avoided also.

Cannabis Blueberry Homemade Icecream

Blueberry Icecream made with Canna milk.

INGREDIENTS

- 2 Cups (Canna) Milk
- 2 Cups Heavy Cream
- 1 Cup Sugar
- 1/4 Tsp Vanilla
- 2 Cups Blueberry Pie Filling
- *Optional* Dash Of Cinnamon

OTHER:

- Icecream Maker
- Big Pot
- Candy Thermometer or Equivalent
- Metal or Glass Bowl
- Strainer

- Cheesecloth or Cheap Dish Rags
- 2-4oz of bud or good quality trim
- 1 Gallon of Whole Milk (Important needs to be Whole Milk for the Fat Content)
- Bag of Ice
- Rock salt

Garlic Herb Butter

Cooking Time: 10 minutes

Servings: Depends on your use

Ingredients:

Directions:

Put your cannabutter at room temperature and mix all ingredients in this butter. You can use a food processor, spoon or fork to mix all ingredients. Mix these ingredients for two minutes, if you are doing with a spoon or fork. If you want to use a food processor, don't overmix it.

Transfer blended butter on a plastic wrap or parchment paper. Roll this butter and wrap it tightly. Put this wrap in a zip-top bag and keep this bag in your freezer. Enjoy this butter with Tomahawk or other meals. You shouldn't heat butter at high temperature because this temperature can affect the taste of butter.

CHAPTER 2
BROWNIES RECIPES

Simple Honey Flavored Decedent CBD Brownies

Serving: 12

Prep Time: 10 minutes

Cook Time: 20 minutes

Ingredients

- 1 whole egg
- 1/3 cup honey
- ¾ cup Cannabutter
- 1 teaspoon vanilla
- 2 tablespoons CBD oil infused coconut oil

- 1/3 cup cocoa powder
- ½ teaspoon baking soda

How To:

1. Pre-heat your oven to 325 degrees F
2. Line an 8x8 inch pan with parchment paper
3. Take a bowl and beat in honey, butter, cannabis coconut oil, vanilla, egg together
4. Keep beating until you have a smooth mixture
5. Gently whisk in cocoa powder and baking soda
6. Pour the batter into your prepared baking pan and even the surface
7. Bake for 20 minutes
8. Remove from oven and let it cool
9. Slice and serve
10. Enjoy!

<u>The Elegant Canna Brownies</u>

Serving: 10-12

Prep Time: 25 minutes

Cook Time: 35 minutes

Ingredients

- 1/8 teaspoon baking powder
- 1/8 teaspoon salt
- 1 teaspoon vanilla extract
- ¼ cup + 2 tablespoons all-purpose flour
- ¼ cup Cannabutter
- ¼ cup unsweetened cocoa powder

- ¾ cup white sugar

- 1 whole egg

How To:

1. Pre-heat your oven to 350 degrees F
2. Prepare an 8 by 8-inch square pan and grease it well
3. Dust with flour
4. Take a large saucepan and place it over medium heat
5. Melt in ¼ cup Cannabutter and remove saucepan form stovetop
6. Take a bowl and add eggs, sugar, and vanilla
7. Add baking powder, salt, flour and cocoa
8. Mix well and pour the mixture into your greased pan
9. Bake for 30-35 minutes
10. Enjoy!

Extremely Fudge Cashew CBD Brownies

Serving: 12

Prep Time: 10 minutes

Cook Time: 35 minutes

Ingredients

- 2 cups cashew butter

- 1 -2 cups dark chocolate chips

- 2 whole eggs

- 1 cup pure maple syrup

- ½ cup cacao powder

- 4 dates, pitted

- 2 teaspoons CBD oil (you can mix this in with the Cashew

butter as well)

- 1 teaspoon pink salt
- 1 teaspoon baking soda

How To:

1. Pre-heat your oven to 350 degrees F
2. Take a large bowl and add maple syrup, dates and blend until creamy
3. Blend in cashew butter and slowly add in vanilla extract and eggs
4. Add cacao, baking soda, CBD oil and ½ teaspoon salt
5. Mix well
6. Add chocolate chips according to your desire and mix well
7. Pour the mixture into an 8x8 parchment lined the pan and even out
8. Bake for 30-35 minutes at 350 degrees F
9. Once done, top with a sprinkle of additional chocolate chips and salt
10. Enjoy!

<u>Special Adult brownies</u>

INGREDIENTS

- 1/4 pound Butter
- 3/4 pound Dark Chocolate
- 1 cup Raw Sugar
- 3 large Eggs
- 1/2 cup Plain Flour
- Nutmeg and Cinnamon
- 2 tablespoons Vanilla

- 2-3 ounces Dried cannabis Leaf (or 1 ounce of bud)

DIRECTIONS

Preheat oven to 350 degrees. Grease 9x13-inch baking dish. Over low heat, melt butter and chocolate, stirring constantly. Once chocolate starts to melt turn off heat and continue to stir. Add spices, sugar, and eggs. Stir mixture until smooth, and add flour, 1/4 cups chopped walnuts (if desired), and powdered cannabis. Stir well (add a dash of milk if necessary) and pour into pan. Bake for 20-25 minutes. Let cool and cut into 16-30 squares.

NOTES

Again, like every recipe, you can use Cannabutter.

Satisfying Coconut Oil Brownies

Serving: 12

Prep Time: 10 minutes

Cook Time: 30 minutes

Ingredients

- ½ cup CBD infused coconut oil
- 1/8 cup coconut oil
- 4 and ½ ounces unsweetened chocolate
- ¾ cup all-purpose flour
- ¾ teaspoon salt
- 1 cup packed brown sugar
- 3 whole eggs
- ½ teaspoon vanilla extract
- 2 tablespoons cocoa powder

How To:

1. Pre-heat your oven to 350 degrees F

2. Take an 8-inch square baking pan and line it with foil

3. Grease with butter

4. Take a saucepan and place it over medium heat, add Canna infused coconut oil and chocolate and melt, let it cool for 5 minutes

5. stir in flour, cocoa powder, and salt into the chocolate mixture

6. Mix well

7. Take another bowl and beat in eggs, vanilla and mix well

8. Pour the egg mixture into the chocolate mix and keep mixing until fully incorporated

9. Pour the mixture into your prepared pan and bake for 25-30 minutes

10. Let it cool and carefully lift the brownies up

11. Slice and enjoy!

Garlic Ganja Mashed Potatoes

INGREDIENTS

- 3-4 large Russet Potatoes,
- Washed, Peeled, and Cubed
- 4 large Garlic Heads
- 3 tablespoons Extra Virgin Olive Oil
- 1 tablespoon Basil
- 1 tablespoon Cracked Black Pepper
- 1 tablespoon Kosher Salt
- 1/4 pint Heavy Cream
- 4-6 ounces Ricotta Cheese
- 4 tablespoons Sweet Butter

- 4 tablespoons Cannabutter

DIRECTIONS

Cut the top 1/2 inch off the garlic heads. Add olive oil to the cut heads and sprinkle with basil. Roast in 420-degree oven for 30-50 minutes. The garlic is done when tender to a fork. Boil the cubed potatoes in salted water until fork tender, drain, and mash lightly. Add butters to potatoes and continue to mash. Add pepper, salt, cream, and cheese and mash until smooth. Squeeze garlic into the mix and whip until smooth.

NOTES

You can crumble bacon into your mashed potatoes for an extra crunch; or for a home-style taste, leave the skin on the potatoes.

Almond Brownies

Cooking Time: 30 minutes

Servings: 8

Ingredients:

Directions:

Prepare an oven at almost 325 F.

Spray cooking oil on the baking pan. Now take one bowl and make a mixture of salt, almond flour, cocoa powder and baking powder. Bring a small saucepan to melt cannabutter and chocolate to make a smooth blend. Now whisk yolks, vanilla, and sweetener in a bowl and transfer this mix in butter and chocolate mixture. Whisk it and add it to the dry ingredients and chocolate chips to mix well. Transfer this batter to a baking pan and bake for 10 minutes or until you get a clean toothpick after poking it into the center. Let it cool, cut and serve.

Hash Brownies

These are a favorited delicious classic amongst the cannabis community. Now you will know how to properly make them for yourself or your friends.

INGREDIENTS:

- ¼ cup of cannabis butter, with ¼ cup butter or ½ cup finely chopped bud with ½ cup butter.

- 1 cup of chocolate chips

- 1 cup sugar

- 2 eggs

- ¾ cups self-rising flour

- 1 ½ teaspoon vanilla

- ¾ cup chopped pecans

DIRECTIONS

Preheat oven to 350 degrees F. Grease a 9 inch square baking pan. Melt butter, cannabis butter(or shake) and 1 cup of chocolate chips in a large saucepan over low heat. Remove it from heat. Stir in the remaining ingredients in the order listed, mixing well. Spread batter in prepared pan and bake for 25 to 30 minutes. Slightly pull away from sides of pan and let cool. Cut into 2 inch squares and enjoy!

The Vegan CBD Brownie

Serving: 24

Prep Time: 10 minutes

Cook Time: 30 minutes

Ingredients

- 4 cups all-purpose flour

- 2 cups cocoa powder

- 3 cups granulated sugar

- 1 and ½ teaspoon salt

- 1 tablespoon baking powder
- 2 cups applesauce
- ½ cup agave nectar
- 1 and ½ cups sunflower oil
- 3 tablespoons CBD oil
- 1 tablespoon vanilla extract
- 2 cups mini chocolate chips
- 6 tablespoons cocoa nibs

How To:

1. Tae a mixing bowl and add all of the dry ingredients
2. Take another bowl and mix all of the wet ingredients
3. Pour the wet ingredients into the dry ingredients and mix well until you have a fine batter
4. Take two 9 x 12 baking pans and line them with parchment paper
5. Lightly grease them with oil
6. Fill them up with your batter and top with cocoa nibs
7. Bake for 12 minutes at 325 degrees F
8. Let the brownies cool and slice them accordingly
9. Serve and enjoy!

CHAPTER 3
COOKIES

America's Classic Chocolate Chip Cookie

Serving: 12

Prep Time: 10 minutes

Cook Time: 30 minutes

Ingredients:

- 3 cups flour
- 1 teaspoon baking soda
- 1 cup white sugar
- 1 cup packed brown sugar
- ½ teaspoon salt
- 2 cups semisweet chocolate chips
- 1 cup prepared Cannabutter
- 2 whole eggs
- 2 teaspoons hot water
- 2 teaspoons vanilla extract
- 1 cup walnuts, chopped

How To:

1. Pre-heat your oven to 350 degrees F
2. Add Cannabutter, brown sugar, white sugar to a bowl and mix well
3. Beat until the mixture is creamy and smooth
4. Beat in one egg at a time, making sure to stir the mixture

after every addition

5. Stir In the vanilla extract

6. Dissolve baking soda in hot water and add to the batter

7. Season with salt

8. Gently add chocolate chips, nuts, and flour

9. Take an ungreased pan and drop large spoonfuls of the mixture into the pan

10. Bake for 30 minutes until edges start to appear golden brown

11. Serve and enjoy!

Toke-House Cookies

INGREDIENTS

- 2 1/4 cups All-Purpose Flour
- 1 teaspoon Baking Soda
- 1 teaspoon Salt
- 1 cup Butter
- 1/2 ounce cannabis
- 3/4 cup Sugar
- 3/4 cup Brown Sugar, Packed
- 1 teaspoon Vanilla Extract
- 1 3/4 cups Chocolate Chips
- 1 cup Nuts, Chopped (Optional)

DIRECTIONS

Melt the Cannabutter in a saucepan over low to medium-low heat. Stir in the chopped cannabis. Continue to stir; if the mixture begins to bubble, reduce heat to low. Simmer for at least 30 minutes, the longer the better. When butter turns green, remove from heat.

Strain the mixture through a section of cheesecloth. Fold up the material into a bag and squeeze the rest of the butter out of the remaining cannabis. In a small bowl, combine the flour, baking soda, and salt. In a larger bowl, beat the Cannabutter, sugar, brown sugar, and vanilla until creamy. Add the eggs, one at a time, beating well after each addition. Gradually beat in the flour mixture. Stir in the chocolate chips and anything else you want like chopped nuts. Using a #20 ice cream scooper, drop the dough on an ungreased baking sheet. Preheat oven to 375 degrees, and bake for 9-11 minutes, or until golden brown. Cool on a wire rack. Recipe makes about 5 dozen cookies.

NOTES

Eat only a couple cookies every 30 minutes until you figure out the right dosage for you. Make sure you have some regular food to eat when you get the munchies.

<u>Sugar-free Cookies</u>

Cooking Time: 30 minutes

Servings: 10 to 15

Ingredients:

Directions:

1. Let an oven preheat at 350 F. Grease a cookie sheet and keep it aside.

2. Take a bowl to blend sweetener, cannabutter, vanilla until the butter becomes soft. Now add water, egg alternative and vinegar. Mix it and add baking powder along with flour and salt. Blend it on low speed to make the dough. Now keep the bowl on the flat surface and split the dough in half and cover each half with a plastic wrap. Keep it in a refrigerator for almost one hour and let the dough chill.

3. After one hour, roll out the dough on the flat and floured surface. Get desired thickness and use a cutter to cut

cookies and set on a baking sheet. Bake it in the oven for 12 minutes to let it light brown. Let it cool on the wire rack before securing it in an airtight jar.

Coma Cookies

INGREDIENTS

- 2 cups All-Purpose Flour
- 1 1/2 cups Steel Cut Oats
- 1 1/2 cups Light Brown Sugar
- 1 cup Granulated Sugar
- 1 cup Cannabutter
- 2 Eggs
- 2 cups Pecans, Chopped
- 1 cup Currants, Organic
- 1 cup Dried Cranberries, Organic
- 1 teaspoon Salt
- 1 teaspoon Baking Soda
- 2-3 tablespoons Bourbon Vanilla
- 1 teaspoon Nutmeg, Ground
- 1 tablespoon Cinnamon, Ground

DIRECTIONS

Sift together the dry ingredients, except for the steel cut oats, and set aside. Cream the Cannabutter and sugars, then add vanilla and mix in the eggs. Don't overwork the butter and sugar or it will break down. Mix dry ingredients with wet ingredients. Mi in oats with a heavy spoon and blend. Fold in the currants, cranberries, and pecans. Chill the batter. Using a #20 ice cream scooper, drop dough onto greased baking pan at 350 degrees for 15-17 minutes.

NOTES

Instead of currants, you can always use raisins.

Cannagranola Bars

INGREDIENTS

- 4 1/2 cups rolled oats
- 1 cup all-purpose flour
- 1 teaspoon baking soda
- 1 teaspoon vanilla extract
- 2/3 cup canna butter, softened
- 1/2 cup honey
- 1/3 cup packed brown sugar
- 2 cups miniature chocolate chips, or chopped dried fruit, and nuts.

DIRECTIONS

Preheat oven to 325 degrees F (165 degrees C). Lightly grease one 9x13 inch pan. In a large mixing bowl combine the oats, flour, baking soda, vanilla, butter or margarine, honey and brown sugar. Stir in the 2 cups assorted chocolate chips, raisins, nuts etc. Lightly press mixture into the prepared pan. Bake at 325 degrees F (165 degrees C) for 18 to 22 minutes or until golden brown. Let cool for 20 minutes then cut into bars. Let bars cool completely in pan before removing or serving. These are great carry along meds.

NOTES

This recipe is really easy to make and tastes great! I've used dried fruits in different combinations. Dried apples, pineapple, dates, raisins, mango, blueberries, just any kind of dried fruit you like can be used in this recipe. I usually replace the chocolate chips with fruit, or split between fruit and chocolate. Dried raspberries and chocolate chip are awesome!

Smooth & Creamy Cocopot Ice Cream

INGREDIENTS

- 6 oz. Swiss chocolate
- 2 1/4 cup custard(pre-made)
- 1 1/4 cup whipped cream, whipped
- 1/4 oz skunk or Northern lights

DIRECTIONS

Melt chocolate using either a microwave or in double boiler. Using a rubber spatula put chocolate in with custard and mix well. Using the rubber spatula fold pre whipped cream into the above mixture. Put all into a plastic container cover and freeze, if in freezer for a long time set out at room temperature for 2-3 mins. Serve 3 scoops on small dessert plate and top with chocolate shavings.

Green rice Krispy Treats

INGREDIENTS

- 3 Tbsp. Cannabutter
- 10 oz marshmallows
- 6 cups crispy rice cereal

DIRECTIONS

1. Line a 13x9 pan with parchment paper or waxed paper.

2. In a large saucepan, heat the cannabutter and marshmallows over medium heat until melted, stirring frequently. Remove from heat and immediately stir in the cereal, using a rubber spatula that's been sprayed with

cooking spray to prevent sticking.

3. Spread marshmallow/rice cereal mix in the prepared pan. Flatten gently with the spatula. Place pan in fridge to cool before cutting into squares.

4. DEVOUR!

<u>Chewy Poppy Seed Cookies</u>

Serving: 36

Prep Time: 15 minutes

Cook Time: 10-12 minutes

Ingredients

- ½ teaspoon baking soda
    - 1 tablespoon orange zest
    - 1 teaspoon orange juice
    - 1 tablespoon poppy seeds
    - ½ cup Cannabutter
    - 2/3 cup sugar
    - 1 and ¼ cup flour
    - 1 whole egg
    - Dash of salt

How To:

1. Pre-heat your oven to 350 degrees F

2. Take a bowl and whisk in sugar, Cannabutter and beat for 2 minutes

3. Add orange zest, orange juice, egg and mix well

4. Take another bowl and sift in baking soda, salt, and flour

5. Add sifted flour mixture into your original egg and orange batter and mix well, fold in poppy seeds

6. Take a teaspoon and transfer mix into a cookie sheet, making sure to keep spaces in between

7. Transfer to oven and bake for 10-12 minutes

8. Once the edges are golden, let them cool and serve

9. Enjoy!

Dreamy Lemon And Thyme Cookies

Serving: 18

Prep Time: 10 minutes

Cook Time: 8-10 minutes

Ingredients

- 1 and ½ cups flour
- ½ cup powdered sugar
- ¾ cup Cannabutter
- 1 tablespoon lemon zest
- ½ teaspoon salt
- 1 teaspoon fresh thyme

How To:

1. Take a bowl and add powdered sugar, Cannabutter

2. Add lemon juice, salt, thyme, zest

3. Mix well and slowly mix in flour

4. Wrap the dough tightly in plastic wrap

5. Transfer to fridge and chill for 1 hour

6. Remove dough and roll it out on your floured surface

7. Roll until it has a thickness of ¼ inch

8. Use cookie cutters to cut it out into shapes

9. Transfer them to a greased baking sheet and transfer to oven

10. Bake for 8-10 minutes

11. Let it cool

12. Serve and enjoy!

Magic Tea Helper

INGREDIENTS

- 1 cup Light Cream
- 1 gram cannabis

DIRECTIONS

In a saucepan over medium-low heat, bring the light cream to almost a boil. Turn off the heat, and add cannabis. Mix in well with a wooden spoon. Cover, and let cool for 1-2 hours. Strain the milk with some cheesecloth, and add to your morning coffee or tea.

NOTES

The amount of cannabis you use, like in any recipe in this book, is entirely up to you. The more the merrier of course!!!

Hash Fudge

INGREDIENTS

- 3/4 cup Heavy Cream
- 2 cups Sugar
- 1 teaspoon Cornstarch
- 2 ounces Unsweetened Chocolate
- 3 grams Hash
- 3 tablespoons Butter
- 1 tablespoon Vanilla

DIRECTIONS

1. In a metal saucepan, combine milk, sugar, chocolate, and cornstarch over medium heat. Stir until the mixture comes to 240 degrees (on a candy thermometer). Immediately remove from heat, and leave the thermometer in. Take 3 tablespoons of butter and melt in microwave. Mix in the hash and stir, put back in microwave for 30 seconds, and stir again. Add the hash-butter mixture into your chocolate mixture, but do not stir! When the temperature of the fudge drops to 110 degrees, use a big spoon and stir vigorously for at least 7 minutes, or until it starts to get difficult to stir. Spread in a baking dish, 9x13 inches will work fine, and let the fudge cool down.

NOTES

To save on cleanup time, line the bottom of your baking dish with aluminum foil. If your fudge doesn't turn out right, you probably weren't using a thermometer or you were too impatient and did not let it cool down. Both are important to making good fudge. You could always use Cannabutter if you do not have hash.

Cannacoffee Milkshake

INGREDIENTS

- 2 cups Vanilla Ice Cream
- 1 cup Whole Milk
- 1 teaspoon Vanilla Extract
- 1 tablespoon Instant Coffee
- 2 grams cannabis

DIRECTIONS

If you have the time, finely chop your cannabis and let it sit overnight in milk. In a blender, combine ice cream, milk and cannabis mixture, vanilla, and instant coffee.

Blend until smooth. Pour into glass and serve.

NOTES

If you don't like coffee, you can always add 1-tablespoon cocoa powder.

Mouth-Watering CBD Snicker Doodles

Serving: 26

Prep Time: 20 minutes

Cook Time: 35 minutes

Ingredients

- 1 teaspoon vanilla extract
- 1 whole egg
- 1 and ½ grams hash
- ½ cup Cannabutter
- ¼ teaspoon baking soda
- ½ teaspoon cream of tartar
- 1 and 1/3 cups all-purpose flour
- 1 and ¾ cups sugar, divided

How To:

1. Pre-heat your oven to 375 degrees F
2. Take a baking sheet and grease it well
3. Take a small bowl and stir in ¼ cup sugar, cinnamon and keep it on the side
4. Take a large bowl and beat in butter, rest of the sugar, and blend for 2 minutes until fluffy
5. Sprinkle ground hash and beat until everything is distributed evenly

6. Beat in egg and vanilla

7. Lower speed to medium-low and mix in flour until blended

8. Scoop out cookies and roll them between your hands to form semi-flat balls

9. Transfer to a prepared baking sheet

10. Bake for 10-12 minutes until lightly brown

11. Serve and enjoy!

The Great No-Bake Toffee Canna Cookies

Serving: 10-12

Prep Time: 25 minutes

Cook Time: 10 minutes

Ingredients

- 1 tablespoons Cannabutter
- 1 cup peanut butter
- 3 cups quick-cooking oats
- ½ cup bittersweet chocolate chips
- ½ cup semi-sweet chocolate chips
- ½ cup toffee bits
- ½ teaspoon salt

How To:

1. Take a baking sheet and line it with wax paper
2. Take a bowl and add oats, chocolate chips, peanut butter, toffee bits,
1. Cannabutter and salt
2. Mix well and transfer mix to a medium sized saucepan
3. Cook over medium heat for about 3-5 minutes until

chocolate melts

4. Scoop a heaping tablespoon of the batter onto your baking sheet

5. Sprinkle toffee bits over each cookie

6. Chill for 15 minutes and serve

7. Enjoy!

Hearty Canna Vanilla Cookies

Serving: 10-12

Prep Time: 20 minutes

Cook Time: 10 minutes

Ingredients

- ¼ teaspoon salt
- ½ teaspoon baking soda
- 1 teaspoon hot water
- 1 teaspoon vanilla extract
- ½ cup softened Cannabutter
- ½ cup white sugar
- ½ cup brown sugar
- 1 cup semisweet chocolate chips
- 1 – ½ cups all-purpose flour
- 1 whole egg

How To:

1. Pre-heat your oven to 350 degrees F

2. Take a bowl and add both sugars, butter and mix well until smooth

3. Add vanilla, egg and mix well

4. Take hot water and stir in baking soda until dissolved

5. Mix the baking soda/hot water mixture into the bowl with sugar and butter, season with salt

6. Add flour and chocolate chips

7. Spoon the mixture into ungreased cookie sheets (small cookie shapes) and bake for 10 minutes until golden

8. Serve and enjoy!

The Purest Butter Cookies Ever!

Serving: 10-12

Prep Time: 15 minutes

Cook Time: 10 minutes

Ingredients

- ¼ teaspoon baking powder
- ¼ teaspoon vanilla extract
- ¼ cup Cannabutter
- 1/3 cup firmly packed brown sugar
- 2/3 cup all-purpose flour
- 1 whole egg

How To:

1. Grease your cookie sheets and keep them on the side

2. Pre-heat your oven to 350 degrees F

3. Thoroughly mix eggs, sugar, vanilla, Cannabutter in a bowl

4. Sift in baking powder, flour and stir well

5. Separate your dough into two-inch square pieces and take the pieces, coat them in brown sugar

6. Transfer the pieces to your prepared cookie sheet (make

sure to leave 2-inch space between them)

7. Bake for 10 minutes until golden brown

8. Serve and enjoy!

The Cookie Paradiso

Serving: 36

Prep Time: 15 minutes

Cook Time: 15 minutes

Ingredients

- 1 teaspoon baking powder
- 1 teaspoon vanilla
- ¼ cup crystallized ginger, chopped
- ½ cup softened Cannabutter
- 1 can (8 ounces) pineapple, with juice, drained
- 2/3 cup macadamia nuts, chopped
- ¾ cup sugar
- ¾ cup sweetened flaked coconut
- 1 and ¾ cup flour

How To:

1. Pre-heat your oven to 350 degrees F
2. Take a large bowl and add Cannabutter, sugar
3. Beat with a whisk until fluffy
4. Add pineapple, vanilla and mix well
5. Add flour, baking powder and beat well
6. Gently stir In nuts, ¼ cup coconut, and crystallized ginger
7. Add remaining coconut in a small bowl

8. Shape your dough into 1 inch balls and dip the top of each cookie intro remaining coconut

9. Take cookies and transfer them to ungreased baking sheets

10. Make sure to keep two-inch space between cookies

11. Bake for 12-15 minutes

12. Let them cool for 5 minutes

13. Serve and enjoy!

Crunchy Peanut Butter Cookies

Serving: 24

Prep Time: 10 minutes

Cook Time: 10-15 minutes

Ingredients

- ½ cup Cannabutter
- 1 cup peanut butter, crunchy
- 2 tablespoons shortening
- 1 whole egg
- 1 teaspoon vanilla
- 1 cup flour
- ½ cup sugar
- ½ teaspoon baking soda
- ½ cup brown sugar
- ½ teaspoon salt

How To:

1. Pre-heat your oven to 350 degrees F

2. Take two baking sheets and grease them, keep them on the side

3. Take a medium bowl and stir in flour, sugar, baking soda, salt and baking powder

4. Mix well and keep it on the side

5. Take another bowl and beat in shortening, Cannabutter, egg, peanut butter, vanilla and mix well

6. Fold the dry ingredients into the wet ingredients (little at a time) and keep mixing until fully incorporated

7. Drop cookie dough using a tablespoon onto your prepared baking sheet

8. Press indents on top using a fork and semi-flatten the cookies

9. Sprinkle salt 1 part salt and 2 parts sugar on top of the cookies

10. Bake for 10-12 minutes until the top begins to crack

11. Remove and serve

12. Enjoy!

Oatmeal Cookies

INGREDIENTS

- 2 extra large Eggs
- 3/4 cup Cannabutter
- 2 cups Raw Sugar
- 2 teaspoons Vanilla Extract
- 1 tablespoon Nutmeg, Ground
- 1 tablespoon Cloves, Ground
- 1 tablespoon Cinnamon, Ground
- 2 cups Whole Wheat Flour
- 1/2 teaspoon Baking Soda
- 1 teaspoon Sea Salt

- 2 tablespoons Water
- 1 1/2 cups Raisins
- 2 cups Rolled Oats
- 1 cup Pecans, Chopped

DIRECTIONS

Cream together the eggs, butter, sugar, and vanilla. Sift the spices, flour, baking soda, and salt into the creamed mixture. Add the water, raisins, oats, and pecans; mix thoroughly. Chill cookie dough for 20 minutes. Using a #20 ice cream scooper, place the dough on a buttered cookie sheet. Top with raw sugar if you want. Bake in preheated 350-degree oven for 12-20 minutes.

NOTES

For a variation, use butterscotch morsels instead of raisins and pecans.

Wake-N-No-Bake Cookies

INGREDIENTS

- 2 cup Sugar
- 1/2 cup Cannabutter • 1/2 cup Milk
- 3 tablespoons Cocoa
- 3 cups Quick Oat
- 1 teaspoon Salt
- 1 teaspoon Vanilla

DIRECTIONS

In a large saucepan, add the sugar, butter, milk, and cocoa. Bring to a rapid boil, and continue to cook for 2 minutes. Remove from heat and add the oats, salt, and vanilla. Using a #20 ice cream scopper, drop onto wax paper and let cool.

NOTES

I suppose you could even microwave this.

The Thin

INGREDIENTS

- 2 1/4 cups All-Purpose Flour
- 1 teaspoon Kosher Salt
- 1 teaspoon Baking Soda
- 1 Egg
- 2 ounces Milk
- 1 1/2 teaspoons Vanilla Extract
- 2 sticks Cannabutter, Unsalted
- 1 cup Sugar
- 1/2 cup Brown Sugar
- 2 cups Semisweet Chocolate Chips

DIRECTIONS

Heat oven to 375-degrees. Sift together the flour, salt, and baking soda in a mixing bowl. Combine the egg, milk, and vanilla and bring to room temperature in another bowl. Cream the Cannabutter in the mixer's work bowl, starting on low speed to soften the butter. Add the sugars. Increase the speed, and cream the mixture until light and fluffy. Reduce the speed and add the egg mixture slowly. Increase the speed and mix until well combined. Slowly add the flour mixture, scraping the sides of the bowl until thoroughly combined. Stir in the chocolate chips. Scoop onto parchment-lined baking sheets using a #20 ice cream scooper, 6 cookies per sheet. Bake for 13 to 15 minutes, checking the cookies after 5 minutes. Rotate the baking sheet for more even browning. Remove the cookies from the pans immediately.

NOTES

Some people like their cookies thin, and this works really well. These 3 cookie recipes (the chewy, the thin, and the puffy) are by Alton Brown of Good Eats on FoodTV. Some people don't know how to make a cookie a certain way, and by changing the flour type, the fat type, the egg ratio, and the sugar ratio, you can achieve your favorite cookie!

<u>Fancy Oatmeal Cookies</u>

Serving: 12

Prep Time: 30 minutes

Cook Time: 15 minutes

Ingredients

- ¼ cup Cannabutter
- 1 cup salted butter, soft
- 2 cups brown sugar
- 2 whole eggs
- 1 and ½ cups all-purpose flour
- 1 teaspoon salt
- ½ teaspoon baking soda
- 3 cups old-fashioned oats
- 2 teaspoons vanilla extract

How To:

1. Pre-heat your oven to 350 degrees F
2. Take a bowl and add brown sugar, butter and beat until fluffy (use an electric mixer if you prefer)
3. Beat in vanilla and add the eggs one at a time, make sure to scrape the bowl after every addition

4. Take a medium bowl and mix in flour, baking soda, salt

5. Transfer the mix to your creamed mixture in 2-3 batches, keep beating after every addition

6. Mix in oats

7. Use the cookie scoop or large tablespoon to drop portions of your mixture onto a prepared baking sheet, making sure to keep a distance of 2 inches between the cookies

8. Bake for 12-13 minutes if you want a chewy cookie!

9. Let them cool for a while and serve

10. Enjoy!

Marijuanna Chili Con Carne

INGREDIENTS

- 2 pinto beans • 1/2 clove garlic.
- 2 cups red wine
- 1/2-cup mushrooms.
- 4 T. chilli powder
- 1 cup of chopped weed.

DIRECTIONS

Soak beans overnight in salt water. In large pot, pour boiling water over beans and simmer for at least an hour, adding more water as needed to keep the beans covered. Next, add all other ingredients, reduce heat and simmer for 3 hours. Serves 10.

Herbal Spaghetti Sauce

INGREDIENTS

- 1 can tomato paste
- 2 tablespoons olive oil

- 1/2 cup chopped onions
- 1/2 cup chopped marijuana
- 1 pinch pepper
- 1 can water (6 oz)
- 1/2 clove minced garlic
- 1 bay leaf
- 1 pinch thyme
- 1/2 teaspoon salt

DIRECTIONS

1. Mix in a large pot, cover and shimmer with frequent stirring for two hours.
2. Serve over spaghetti. Yummm.

Ganja Gooey balls

INGREDIENTS

- 1 1/2 cups Cannabutter
- 3 cups Oats
- 1/4 cup Peanut Butter
- 3 tablespoons Honey
- 2 teaspoons Cinnamon
- 1-2 tablespoons Cocoa Powder

DIRECTIONS

Melt the Cannabutter in a microwave safe bowl. In a large bowl, combine the oats, peanut butter, honey, cinnamon, and cocoa. Pour the Cannabutter on top and stir until the mixture becomes homogeneous. Place the bowl into the freezer for 10-20 minutes.

Form the mixture into individual balls, using your hands or a #20 ice cream scooper, and drop them onto wax paper to set.

NOTES

Try adding chopped walnuts, raisins, or crisped rice to add a little spin to the recipe. If the result is too gooey, add more oats; if it's too dry, add more peanut butter or honey.

CHAPTER 3
CAKES

Hearty CBD Lemon Bars

Serving: 48 servings

Prep Time: 10 minutes

Cook Time: 30-40 minutes

Ingredients

For Crust

- 2 cups flour
- ½ cup white sugar
- 1 cup Cannabutter
- For Lemon Curd
- ¼ cup flour
- 2 cups sugar
- 4 whole eggs
- 3 lemon, juiced

How To:

1. Pre-heat your oven to 350 degrees F
2. Take a bowl and mix crust ingredients
3. Press crust mix into an ungreased 9x13 inch pan
4. Bake for 15-20 minutes until slightly golden
5. Take a bowl and beat in remaining flour, sugar
6. Take another bowl and beat in lemon juice and eggs

7. Add egg mixture to dry ingredients and stir for 1 minute

8. Take the crust out once ready and pour the lemon mixture over crust

9. Transfer back to oven and bake for 20 minutes

10. Remove and let it cool

11. Serve and enjoy!

Baked Turtle Cheesecake

INGREDIENTS

- 2 c Vanilla Wafer Crumbs
- 1 c Chopped Pecans, Toasted
- 0.25 oz Ganja (processed in spice or coffee grinder)
- 2 ea Large Eggs
- 5 oz (1 cn) Evaporated Milk
- 1 ts Vanilla
- 14 oz Carmels (1 bag)
- 0.5 cup Sugar
- 6.0 tb Margarine, Melted
- 16.0 oz Cream Cheese, Softened
- 0.50 c Semi-sweet Chocolate Chips (chocolate chips should be melted).

DIRECTIONS

Combine crumbs and margarine press onto bottom and sides of 9-inch spring- form pan. Bake at 350 degrees F for 10 minutes. In 1 1/2-quart heavy saucepan, melt caramels with milk over low heat, stirring frequently, until smooth. Pour over crust. Top with pecans and ganja. Combine cream cheese, sugar and vanilla, mixing at medium speed on electric mixer until well blended. Add eggs, one at a time, mixing well after each addition. Blend in chocolate and pour over pecans. Bake at 350 degrees F for 40 minutes. Loosen cake from rim of pan; cool before removing rim of pan. Chill.

NOTES

Garnish with whipped cream, additional chopped nuts and maraschino cherries, if desired. Makes 10 servings.

Sensational Canna Cobbler

Serving: 16

Prep Time: 10 minutes

Cook Time: 40-50 minutes

Ingredients

- ½ cup melted Cannabutter
- ¾ cup Cannamilk
- 1 cup flour
- 1 and ¼ cup white sugar
- ½ cup brown sugar
- ¼ teaspoon baking powder
- ¼ teaspoon salt
- 1 teaspoon baking powder
- ¼ teaspoon cinnamon
- ¼ teaspoon nutmeg
- 7 fresh peaches, chopped
- 1 whole egg
- Peach filling

How To:

1. Pre-heat your oven to 375 degrees F

2. Pour melted Cannabutter into 9x13 inch baking dish

3. Add flour, baking powder, 1 cup white sugar, salt to a bowl

4. Mix well and add Cannamilk, eggs and stir until everything is moist

5. Pour the mix over Cannabutter (do not stir)

6. Take a saucepan and place it over high heat, add spices, brown sugar, fresh peaches, peach filling and remaining white sugar

7. Heat it up and keep stirring until it comes to a boil

8. Remove heat and carefully spread the mixture over the Cannabutter

9. Do not stir

10. Let it bake for 45 minutes until it turns golden and rises

11. Let it cool, serve and enjoy!

Custard Pie

Cooking Time: 50 minutes

Servings: 4

Ingredients:

Directions:

Prepare an oven in advance at 425 F. Whisk eggs to make foam and mix salt, sweetener, vanilla, cannabutter and cream. Mix it well and pour into a greased pie plate. Sprinkle nutmeg before keeping it in the oven to bake for 10 minutes. After 10 minutes, reduce the oven to 325 and cook for 30 minutes again. To keep the crust moist and downy, make sure to add a pan of water to the bottom of the rack. Check the pie with a toothpick, if it comes out clean and let it chill and enjoy.

Hazy Lemon Bars

Serving: 10-12

Prep Time: 15 minutes

Cook Time: 40 minutes

Ingredients

- 1/8 teaspoon baking powder
- 1 tablespoon + 1 and ½ teaspoon all-purpose flour
- 2 tablespoons + 1 and ¾ teaspoon lemon juice
- 3 tablespoons white sugar
- ¼ cup + 2 tablespoons soft Cannabutter
- 1 cup all-purpose flour
- 1 to 2 whole eggs
- ½ cup + 1 tablespoons white sugar

How To:

12. Pre-heat your oven to 350 degrees F
13. Take a bowl and add butter, sugar, flour and mix well to prepare the crust
14. Transfer the mixture to your 8-inch square pan and press the mixture evenly
15. Bake for 20 minutes until the crust turns crispy
16. Take a bowl and blend in 2 tablespoons flour, baking powder, sugar, lemon juice and combine well
17. Pour the mixture over your pre-baked crust and transfer it back to your oven
18. Bake for 20 minutes
19. Let it cool and top with powdered sugar
20. Serve and enjoy!

Basil And Strawberry CBD Infused Cake

Serving: 10-12

Prep Time: 10 minutes

Cook Time: 10-15 minutes

Ingredients

- 10 ounces crème Fraiche
- 2 teaspoons balsamic vinegar
- 1/8 cup brown sugar
- ½ cup sugar
- Strawberries, sliced
- 2 ounces sweet wine
- Basil leaves
- 2 cups flour
- 2/3 cup almonds
- 1 cup Cannabutter

How To:

1. Take a bowl and add brown sugar, vinegar, crème Fraiche
2. Transfer to fridge
3. Pre-heat your oven to 350 degrees F
4. Process almonds in food processor and break them down into crumbs
5. Take a bowl and mix in butter and white sugar, blend until creamy
6. Add flour, processed almonds, salt to a bowl and mix until a dough begins to form
7. Roll dough and cut into your desired pieces
8. Transfer them to a baking sheet and transfer the sheet to

your oven

9. Bake for 10 minutes until light brown

10. Take them out and let them cool

11. Take a bowl and soak cut strawberries in sweet wine for 5 minutes

12. Take out the crème Fraiche mix

13. Add soaked strawberry slices to your crème Fraiche mix ice the cakes with the mixture if you prefer

14. Garnish with basil and enjoy!

15. Alternatively, you can garnish your cakes with the sliced strawberries and basil and serve with the crème Fraiche as dippers

Amazing Canna Carrot Cake

Serving: 12

Prep Time: 25 minutes

Cook Time: 1 hour 5 minutes

Ingredients

- 1 cup Cannamilk
- 3 whole eggs
- 1 and ½ cups sugar
- 2 teaspoons baking soda
- 2 cups all-purpose flour
- 2 cups carrots, shredded
- 1 cup flaked coconut
- 1 cup walnuts, chopped
- 1 can (14.5 ounces) crushed pineapple, with juice
- 1 cup raisins

- 2 teaspoons vanilla extract
- 2 teaspoons ground cinnamon
- ¼ teaspoon salt

How To:

1. Pre-heat your oven to 350 degrees F
2. Take an 8 x 12-inch pan and grease it well
3. Dust with flour
4. Take a medium bowl and sift in flour, salt, cinnamon and baking soda
5. Keep the mixture on the side
6. Take a large bowl and add eggs, oil, Cannamilk, vanilla, and sugar
7. Mix well
8. Add flour mixture and stir
9. Take a medium bowl and add carrots, walnuts, coconut, pineapples, and raisins
10. Take a large spoon and whisk in the carrot mix into the batter and fold
11. Pour the mixture into your prepared 8 x 12-inch pan
12. Bake for 1 hour until a toothpick comes out clean
13. Let it cool and serve
14. Enjoy!

Purple Cake

Cooking Time: 40 minutes

Servings: 8 to 12

Ingredients:

Directions:

1. Preheat an oven to almost 400°F.

2. Blend the cake mix according to the instructions given on the package. Use cannabis infused oil instead of ordinary cooking oil. Mix water and eggs and whisk this mixture well.

3. Pour this batter into two pans of equal size and bake for almost 30 minutes in a preheated oven. Check with a toothpick, if it comes out clean, the cake is ready.

4. Mix up your vanilla frosting with a few drops of purple food color and spread it on the top of one cake. Put the second cake on the top to make a sandwich. Frost your entire cake and enjoy chilled.

Chocolate Cake

Cooking Time: 50 minutes

Servings: 8

Ingredients:

Directions:

1. Let the oven heat in advance at 300° F or (150° C).

2. It is time to blend eggs and tagatesse to make it smooth. Now mix milk, CannaButter, almond flour, cocoa and coconut flour in a bowl. It is time to sprinkle husk and baking powder, marmalade, apricots, and berries in this bowl. Mix all the ingredients.

3. Now take a loaf pan to grease it and transfer batter to the baking pan to bake it for 40 to 50 minutes. It is time to melt chocolate and heavy cream. Spread this blend on the top of the cake and let it cool. Now decorate the cake with berries, lemon balm, and apricots.

Elegant Canna Pancakes

Serving: 6

Prep Time: 5 minutes

Cook Time: 10 minutes

Ingredients

- ½ cup whole milk
- ½ cup Cannamilk
- 1 cup all-purpose flour
- 2 tablespoons white sugar
- 2 teaspoons baking powder
- 2 tablespoons vegetable oil
- 1 whole egg, beaten
- 1 teaspoon salt

How To:

1. Take a large sized bowl and add flour, sugar, salt and baking powder
2. Make a well in the center and pour Cannamilk, egg, oil and whole milk
3. Mix well until the batter is smooth
4. Take a frying pan and lightly oil it, place it over medium-high heat
5. Pour a scoop of the batter and gently cook brown both sides
6. Repeat until the whole batter has been used up, try to use an approximately ¼ cup of the batter for a single pancake
7. Serve and enjoy!

The Great One-Pan Pot Lemon Cake

Serving: 9

Prep Time: 15 minutes

Cook Time: 30 minutes

Ingredients

Cake

- ½ teaspoon salt
- 1 and ½ teaspoon baking powder
- 2 teaspoons fresh lemon zest, grated
- ¼ cup Cannabutter
- ¾ cup milk
- 1 cup sugar
- 1 and ¼ cups flour
- 1 whole egg

Glaze

- 1 tablespoon melted Cannabutter
- 2-3 teaspoons lemon juice
- ¾ cup powdered sugar
- Lemon zest

How To:

1. Pre-heat your oven to 350 degrees F
2. Prepare an 8x8 baking pan and grease it
3. Add dry ingredients to the baking pan and mix
4. Make a hole in the middle
5. Take a bowl and add lemon zest, eggs, and stir
6. Pour the mixture into the well and add melted Cannabutter
7. Pour milk over the entire mix

8. Stir well

9. Bake for 30 minutes until a toothpick comes out clean from the center

10. Take a bowl and add 1 tablespoon Cannabutter, lemon juice, and powdered sugar

11. Mix well to create the glaze

12. Once the cake is baked and cooled, spread the glaze over the cake

13. Slice and serve

14. Enjoy!

Canna Infused Blueberry Cheesecake Delight

Serving: 10

Prep Time: 20 minutes

Cook Time: 70-80 minutes

Ingredients

- 1 cup crumbled Graham Crackers
- 3 tablespoons flour
- 3 whole eggs
- 2 tablespoons melted Cannabutter
- 1 cup + 1 tablespoon sugar
- 8 ounces + ¼ cup sour cream
- 3 blocks of 8 ounces each, cream cheese
- ½ teaspoon salt
- 1 teaspoon vanilla extract
- 1 cup cool Whip cream
- 2 cups blueberries

- 1 teaspoon lemon extract

How To:

1. Pre-heat your oven to 350 degrees F

2. Add Graham crackers to a food processor and combine with melted butter, 3 tablespoons sugar

3. Process until crumbly

4. Press the mixture into the bottom of your pie pan and bake for 5 minutes

5. Remove and let it cool

6. The lower temperature of the oven to 325 degrees F

7. Take a bowl and beat in soft cream cheese, 1 cup sugar, salt, flour

8. Add eggs one at a time until mixed well

9. Add the extracts and sour cream

10. Mix well

11. Fold in blueberries and pour the mixture into cooled crust

12. Bake for 50 minutes at 325 degrees F

13. Remove heat and let it sit in oven (door open) for 20 minutes

14. Cover and let it chill

15. Serve and enjoy with a mixture of cool whip and remaining the sour cream

Milk Chocolate Chip Cookies

INGREDIENTS

- 2 cups Flour

- 1/2 teaspoon Baking Soda

- 1/2 teaspoon Salt

- 1 cup Cannabutter
- 2/3 cup Sugar
- 2/3 cup Brown Sugar, Lightly Packed
- 1 Egg
- 1 teaspoon Vanilla
- 1 package Milk Chocolate Chips

DIRECTIONS

Cream together Cannabutter and sugars. Beat in egg, and add vanilla. Sift dry ingredients into creamed mixture, and fold in milk chocolate chipes. Bake 8-10 minutes in prehated 375-degree oven.

NOTES

Dark chocolate chunks sounds pretty good too!

The Chewy

INGREDIENTS

- 2 sticks Cannabutter, Unsalted
- 2 1/4 cups Bread Flour
- 1 teaspoon Kosher Salt
- 1 teaspoon Baking Soda • 1/4 cup Sugar
- 1 1/4 cups Brown Sugar
- 1 Egg
- 1 Egg Yolk
- 2 tablespoons Milk
- 1 1/2 teaspoons Vanilla Extract
- 2 cups Semisweet Chocolate

DIRECTIONS

Preheat oven to 375-degrees. Melt butter in a heavy-bottom

medium saucepan over low heat. Sift together the flour, salt, and baking soda and set aside. Pour the melted butter in the mixer's bowl. Add the sugar and brown sugar. Cream the butter and sugars on medium speed. Add the egg, yolk, milk, and vanilla and mix until well combined. Slowly incorporate flour mixture. Fold in chocolate chips. Chill the dough, then scoop onto parchment-lined baking sheets using a #20 ice cream scooper; 6 cookies per sheet. Bake for 14 minutes, or until golden brown, checking the cookies after 5 minutes. Rotate the baking sheet for even browning.

NOTES

This is the best recipe I have used for making cookies that are nice and chewy. The secret is the use of an egg and an egg yolk; also, chilling the dough is important.

The Puffy

INGREDIENTS

- 1 cup Cannashortening, Butter Flavored
- 3/4 cup Sugar
- 1 cup Brown Sugar
- 2 1/4 cups Cake Flour
- 1 teaspoon Kosher Salt
- 1 1/2 teaspoons Baking Powder
- 2 Eggs
- 1 1/2 teaspoons Vanilla Extract
- 2 cups Semisweet Chocolate Chips

DIRECTIONS

Heat oven to 375-degrees. Combine the Cannashortening, sugar, and brown sugar in the mixer's work bowl, and cream until light and fluffy. In the meantime, sift together the cake flour, salt, and baking powder and set aside. Add the eggs 1 at a time to the creamed mixture. Then add vanilla. Increase the speed until thoroughly incorporated. With the mixer set to low, slowly add the dry ingredients to the shortening and combine well. Stir in the chocolate chips. Chill the dough. Scoop onto parchment-lined baking sheets using a #20 ice cream scooper, 6 per sheet. Bake for 13 minutes or until golden brown and puffy, checking the cookies after 5 minutes. Rotate the baking sheet for even browning.

NOTES

The secret behind a big puffy cookie is the use of cake flour, shortening, and the mix of brown to white sugars.

Ultimate Canna-Flavored Banana Bread

Serving: 10

Prep Time: 10 minutes

Cook Time: 60-70 minutes

Ingredients

- 2 cups flour
- ¼ cup plain yogurt
- ½ cup melted Cannabutter
- 2 whole eggs
- 4 mashed ripe bananas
- 1 teaspoon vanilla extract
- ½ teaspoon salt
- ¾ teaspoon baking soda
- 1 cup whole, toasted walnuts, chopped
- ¼ cup Cannabis, ground

How To:

1. Pre-heat your oven to 350 degrees F

2. Grease a 9x5 inch bread loaf pan

3. Dust with flour

4. Take a bowl and mix in baking soda, ground cannabis, sugar and flour

5. Take another bowl and beat in eggs, Cannabutter, vanilla, mashed bananas, yogurt and mix well

6. Take the wet ingredients and slowly fold them into dry ingredients until combined

7. The batter should be chunky and thick

8. Fold in walnuts and gently beat

9. Scrape the batter into loaf pan and bake for 60 minutes

10. Remove from oven and let it cool

11. Slice and serve

12. Enjoy!

Lovely Chocolate Dredged No-Bake Oreo Cake

Serving: 12

Prep Time: 20-30 minutes + Overnight chill time

Cook Time: Nil

Ingredients

- 1 cup chocolate syrup

- 4 tablespoons Cannabutter

- 3 packs (8 ounces each) cream cheese, at room temperature

- 2 packs Oreos, wafers

How To:

1. Take 20 of your Oreo cookies and transfer them to a plastic bag, crush them into fine crumbs

2. Line an 8-inch cake pan with plastic wrap and let about 5 inches hang over sides of the pan

3. Take a bowl and beat cream cheese until fluffy

4. Beat in butter and chocolate syrup until smooth

5. Circularly arrange whole cookies along the bottom of your cake pan

6. Spoon 1 and ¼ cups of chocolate cream over cookies

7. Keep layering cookies and chocolate cream mix until all mixture has been used up

8. You should have 4 layers

9. Once layering it done, cover pie with the excess plastic wrap hanging on the sides

10. Tap onto the countertop surface to even things out and transfer to your fridge

11. Let it chill overnight

12. Once chilled, peel the plastic wrap and cut into wedges

13. Serve and enjoy!

CHAPTER 4
CANNABIS SOUPS

Fish Bone Broth

Cooking Time: 24 hours

Servings: 3 to 4

Ingredients:

Directions:

Melt cannabutter In a large stainless steel pot and cook vegetables to make them soft. Now add the white wine to let it boil.

It is time to add fish carcasses and cover with water. Now add vinegar and let it boil. Remove any fat and foam that may float on the top of the broth during cooking.

Now add dry or fresh thyme and parsley to the pot and reduce the heat. Cover it to cook for 4 hours to 24 hours. Once it is done, strain the liquid and secure it in containers or jars. You can keep it in the freezer or fridge.

Chicken Soup

Cooking Time: 6 to 8 hours

Servings: 4 to 5

Ingredients:

Directions:

Mix all the ingredients in a slow cooker and mix them to combine. Cover this cooker for almost 6 to 8 hours on a low setting and serve with Cannabutter at the top.

Beef and Vegetable Soup

Cooking Time:

Servings: 4 to 6

Ingredients:

Directions:

Mix the beef, water, carrot, broth, parsnips, onion, parmesan, celery, curry powder, salt and black pepper in a slow cooker. Cook it on a low setting for almost 8 hours and then remove the meat from the cooker. Let it cool and shred the meat. Add it to the soup with peas and dill, sprinkle salt and pepper on it. Squeeze lemon while serving in the soup bowls. Top with cannabutter and serve.

Sausages and Cabbage Soup

Cooking Time: 2 ½ hours

Servings: 4 to 6

Ingredients:

Cabbage Soup and Sausages

Direction:

1. Heat olive oil in a pan over medium heat and add chopped sausages to cook it for a few minutes. Add cabbage, onion, carrots, caraway seeds, garlic, celery salt, water and broth in the crock pot. Cook on a high setting for two hours, but keep stirring it.

2. Now add remaining seasoning in the pan and mix it well. You need to cook it for almost three more hours to tender all the vegetables. Serve hot with Cannabutter!

Thai Vegan Soup

Cooking Time: 35 minutes

Servings: 4 to 5

Ingredients:

Directions:

1. Take a pot and sauté cannabis for almost 10 minutes. Mix them frequently and slowly add lemongrass and mango juice. Let it cook for nearly five minutes.

2. Add water chestnuts, corn, basil, green onions, mint, cilantro, garlic, curry powder, hot sauce, and ginger. Mix frequently and cook for almost 15 minutes.

3. Add lime juice, one pinch salt and sesame oil. Discard lemon grass before serving. Serve in small bowls and add one tablespoon of THC oil in every bowl.

CHAPTER 5
BEVERAGES

Jamaican Recipe

Cooking Time: 5 minutes

Servings: 2

Ingredients:

Directions:

Take the desired amount of cannabis oil or tincture and mix with rum. Combine this rum, coconut water, and Amaretto and shake them well. Strain in a cup over ice.

Crispy Morning Shake

Cooking Time: 5 minutes

Servings: 2

Ingredients:
Directions:

Add all these ingredients in a blender and blend them well. Pour into a glass and drink cold.

Cannabis Elixir
INGREDIENTS

- cannabis Tincture
- Honey

- 4-6 Vitamin E Capsules

DIRECTIONS:

Place the tincture in a double boiler over an electric heat source. Reduce the solution by half. Once reduce, add 1/2 the remaining volume of tincture in honey along with the vitamin E capsules (e.g. if you have 2 quarts of tincture after reduction, you would add 1 quart honey). Continue to reduce the volume with constant stirring until you have nearly boiled it down to the original volume of syrup you began with. Let cool, and store in a lightproof glass in the refrigerator.

NOTES

The dosage should be between a teaspoon and a couple tablespoons. You can customize your elixirs by adding different herbs, like adding syrup of Elderberry makes an effective treatment for influenza; or adding Kava can provide greater pain control and sedation. With a little study in herbal medicine, you can customize your blends for any ailment. For the flu, use cannabis tincture with Elderberry and Cat's Claw.

Magic Tincture

INGREDIENTS

- 2-3 tablespoons Honey
- 1/2 ounce cannabis
- 3 ounces Vodka
- 1 teaspoon Ginger, Grated
- 1 teaspoon Orange Zest

DIRECTIONS

In a small saucepan, heat honey over low heat. Do not let the honey foam over! Mix in the powdered cannabis, and while stirring slowly add the Vodka so the texture stays in a liquid form, not a solid sticky mass. Continue to cook over low heat for 30 minutes. Pour into a jar and cover, let sit in the refrigerator until cool.

NOTES

Take a teaspoon every 15 minutes until you figure out a "dose" that is good for you.

Hot Buttered Blast

INGREDIENTS

- 1/8 pound Butter
- 1/2 ounce cannabis
- 8 ounces Vodka
- 1 tablespoon Honey

DIRECTIONS

In a medium saucepan, melt 1/8 pound of butter over medium heat. Add the cannabis, which should be ground up into a fine powder. Add the Vodka and bring the mixture to a boil, stirring the entire time. Once boiling, reduce to medium-low heat and let sit for 10-30 minutes, or overnight. Strain the mixture and let cool to room temperature. Add honey to taste, and pour into a glass.

NOTES

You could always use a 1/4 ounce of cannabis if you are not up to the intense trip of a half ounce. Substitute Vodka with Everclear for a stronger kick.

Cannamelon

INGREDIENTS

- 1 large Watermelon
- 1/2 ounce cannabis
- 1/5 liter Vodka

DIRECTIONS:

Grind the cannabis to a fine powder. Put the cannabis in a bottle of Vodka, and cover the top of the bottle with cheesecloth and a rubber band. Cut a hole in the watermelon so you can insert the top of the bottle. Put the bottle in the hole and let sit in the refrigerator overnight.

NOTES

This one is great for picnics!

Green Dream

INGREDIENTS

- 1/4 to 1/2 ounce cannabis
- 1/5 liter Vodka

DIRECTIONS:

Grind the cannabis to a fine powder. Put into bottle of vodka and let sit for 2-10 weeks, shaking daily. Add 1 tablespoon of lemon or orange zest for a unique zing!

NOTES

Serve chilled, in a chilled glass with 3 ice cubes, 1 shot of Green Dragon, 3 shots 7UP, and a teaspoon of honey.

<u>Bhang Lassi</u>

INGREDIENTS

- 1/2 ounce cannabis
- 1 cup Water
- 2 cups Whole Milk, Warm
- Pinch of Garam Masala
- 1 tablespoon Coconut Milk
- 1 tablespoon Almonds, Chopped
- 1/8 teaspoon Powdered Ginger
- 1/2 cup Sugar
- 1/2 teaspoon Sugar Water and Grenadine

DIRECTIONS:

Boil water in teapot and add the cannabis. Brew for 7-10 minutes, then strain. Squeeze any remaining liquids out of leftover cannabis. Save cannabis for later, in separate bowl. Grind the bud and 2 tablespoons of milk together, slowly. Do this about 4 times. Stick the milk in a bowl, and take the cannabis out. Add the cannabis and a bit more milk and grind it some more, adding the almonds. Squeeze the bud and repeat several times. Discard the remaining cannabis, and add all the liquids together (milk, coconut milk, sugar water, and water from the tea). Then add the spices, stir.

NOTES

Use an old teapot unless you want your house to smell like cannabis every time you want coffee. It will also smell a lot when you are brewing. This is a drink that the novice user should definitely avoid, especially if you don't like the effects from eating cannabis.

Pot Hot Chocolate

INGREDIENTS

- 1 cup Whole Milk
- 1 cup Light Cream
- 4 grams cannabis
- 5 ounces Unsweetened Chocolate
- 1/2 teaspoon Vanilla
- 5 tablespoons Sugar
- Pinch of Salt
- Pinch of Cinnamon

DIRECTIONS

Combine the milk, sugar, and salt in a saucepan on medium heat. Once the salt and sugar has dissolved, add the light cream, cinnamon, vanilla, and finely chopped cannabis. Heat to just under boiling, and add the chocolate. Turn the heat off, and stir until the chocolate has melted. Serve in a mug, and top with whipped cream and orange zest, or stick to the classical miniature marshmallows.

NOTES

For every 8 ounces of milk, whole milk contains 8 grams of fat, 2% milk contains 5 grams of fat, 1% contains 2.5 grams of fat, and skim milk contains no fat. Do not confuse hot cocoa and hot chocolate. While hot cocoa is made from cocoa powder, it lacks the fat of cocoa butter; hot chocolate, however, is made from chocolate bars melted into cream. Unsweetened chocolate is also called baking or bitter chocolate, you could substitute with semi-sweet chocolate, but leave the vanilla out if you do.

Golden Delight

Cooking Time: 22 minutes

Servings: 2

Ingredients:

Directions:

Put all these ingredients in a blender except cannabutter and blend them to make a smooth mixture. Pour this liquid into a saucepan and let it heat. Mix occasionally and cook on low heat for almost 5 – 7 minutes. Pour this mixture into two mugs and top with one teaspoon cannabutter. Serve.

Energetic Smoothie

Cooking Time: 5 minutes

Servings: 2

Ingredients:

Directions:

Put all ingredients in a blender and blend them well to get a smooth texture. Enjoy chilled.

Cannabis Watermelon Juice

Cooking Time: 20 minutes

Servings: 2

Ingredients:

Directions:

Peel watermelon and cut the fruit into small cubes. Add it into a blender along with lemon juice, sugar, and water. Blend them for almost 30 seconds and filter the watermelon juice through your fine sieve into a pitcher. Discard the pulp and mix cannabis tincture along with mint leaves in watermelon juice. Chill in your refrigerator before serving.

CHAPTER 6
SNACKS

Wholesome CBD Marshmallow Munchies

Serving: 20

Prep Time: 10 minutes

Cook Time: 5-10 minutes

Ingredients

- 6 ounces mini marshmallows
- 8 cups crispy rice cereal
- 3 tablespoons Cannabutter
- 1 stick + 1 tablespoons regular unsalted butter

How To:

1. Take a 9-inch square dish and line it with parchment paper
2. Take a small saucepan and place it over medium heat, add butter and let it melt
3. Add Cannabutter and stir over medium-low heat
4. Add marshmallows once the butter has melted and stir gently until incorporated fully
5. Pour crispy rice cereal in a big bowl and gently pour the sticky mixture from the stove over rice cereal
6. Once covered, press the mixture into your prepared pan and let it sit for 30 minutes
7. Slice into squares once cooled an serve
8. Enjoy!

Magical Canna Banana Medley

Serving: 6

Prep Time: 10 minutes

Cook Time: 5 minutes

Ingredients

- 1 pound milk chocolate
- 3 large bananas
- ½ cup Cannabutter

How To:

1. Prepare your double boiler over the stove top and add Cannabutter, let it melt over medium-low heat
2. Pour into a heatproof container and keep it on the side
3. Add chocolate to the double boiler and melt it
4. Once the chocolate has melted, add Cannabutter back to the chocolate and mix well
5. Cut bananas to 1 inch round slices and dip each Banana slice into chocolate
6. Transfer into wax parchment paper and let it cool
7. Once chilled, enjoy!

Fire Crackers

INGREDIENTS

- Ground Marijuana
- Peanut Butter
- Cooking Oil
- 6 Ritz Bits Crackers(can substitute)

DIRECTIONS

Spread a thin layer of peanut butter on all 6 crackers, just enough so its not doesn't smush out the sides when you put them together. Sprinkle your weed evenly on 3 of the crackers. Next dab your oil/melted butter on all 6 of the crackers. Place crackers on top of one each other to make a "sandwich" and wrap indivudualy in tinfoil, airtight! Pop them in the oven at 320F for approximately 25 minutes. Unwrap and let cool for 5-10 mintues and indulge!

Ganja Goodness

INGREDIENTS

- 1 package Miniature Marshmallows
- 1 cup Raw Whole Almonds
- 1 cup Golden Raisins
- 1 cup Dark Raisins
- 3 tablespoons Honey
- 1/4 teaspoon Cinnamon
- 1 teaspoon Vanilla
- 1/4 cup Vegetable Oil
- 4 tablespoons Cannabutter

DIRECTIONS

1. Pour vegetable oil into square pan and spread around bottom and sides. Allow extra oil to remain in pan. Chop up almonds until consistency is of grainy sand. Pout almonds into a pan over medium-high heat. Stir with a wooden spoon for 15 minutes. Keep stirring, do not let them burn. Remove almonds to mixing bowl. Chop the golden and dark raisins into small pieces and mix with almonds. Place Cannabutter in microwave safe bowl and microwave on high for 30 seconds, or until butter is melted. In the same bowl, add miniature marshmallows and microwave for 60

seconds, stir, and microwave for 30-60 seconds more until both combine into a smooth consistency. Add the

2. Cannabutter and marshmallow mixture with the almond and raisin mixture, and fold together with a wooden spoon. Add honey, vanilla, and cinnamon and continue to stir. Pour entire mixture into a square cake pan and press out towards edges. Let sit in fridge for an hour. Slice in 1-square inch sections.

NOTES

Sprinkle confectioners sugar onto each square for an added taste!

Marijuana Meatloaf

INGREDIENTS

- 1/4 ounce cannabis
- 1 pound Medium Lean Ground Beef
- 1 large Egg
- 1/2 package Crushed Saltines
- 1 packet Lipton's Tomato Cup-A-Soup
- 1/2 cup Green Pepper, Chopped
- 1/2 cup Onion, Chopped
- 1 Loaf Pan

DIRECTIONS

Preheat oven to 350 degrees. In a large bowl, combine ground beef, onion, and green pepper. Mix together well with hands. Next, add saltines, soup, and cannabis. Roll the beef into a ball and gouge a hole in it with your thumb. Drop the egg in, combining the ingredients until mixed thoroughly. Spread into loaf pan and place in oven for 20-30 minutes.

NOTES

Don't forget to add some ketchup on top at the end, just like mom used to make!

Scooby Snacks

INGREDIENTS

- 2 cups flour
- 2 eggs
- 1 cup Quaker dry oatmeal
- 1 tbsp vanilla
- 1/2 cup cocoa
- 1/2 cup sugar
- 1/4 pound (1 stick) butter
- 1 tbsp walnut extract
- 1 oz. of finely ground cannabis

DIRECTIONS

Preheat oven to 350 degrees. Combine all ingredients in a large mixing bowl. If there is not enough liquid to mix all ingredients after 5 minutes of stirring, add a tiny amount of milk to aid in mixing of remaining ingredients. Taste batter before cooking and adjust amount of sugar to your liking. Place on a lightly greased cookie sheet and bake for 8 to 12 minutes, depending on how large you made your cookies. Can be cooked for a shorter time for chewier cookies, or a longer time for drier, crisp cookies.

NOTES

It is advisable not to drive after ingesting. In fact, forget about anything you had planned for that day.

Wake-N-Bake Breakfast Sandwiches

INGREDIENTS

- 1-2 grams cannabis
- 2 slices Bread(preferably an English Muffin)
- 2 large Eggs
- 2 slices Bacon
- 2 slices Velveeta Cheese

DIRECTIONS

In a large pan, cook the bacon and scrambled eggs. Assemble the sandwich as follows: 1 slice of bread, buttered side up; 1 gram finely chopped cannabis; 1 slice cheese; 1 slice bacon; scrambled eggs; 1 slice bacon; 1 slice cheese; remaining cannabis; and 1 slice of bread. Press the sandwich together and microwave for 30 seconds, or until cheese has melted.

NOTES

For a lighter version, you could always use butter the bread with Cannabutter.

Apple Buds

INGREDIENTS

- 4 Apples, Cored
- 1/4 cup Butter
- 1/2 cup Brown Sugar

- 1/4 cup Water
- 1/3 cup cannabis
- 2 tablespoons Cinnamon

DIRECTIONS

Finely chop the cannabis until it is a powder. In a food processor or blender, mix in cannabis, butter, sugar, and warm water. Stuff cored apples with cannabis mixture. Sprinkle apples with cinnamon, and top with a cherry. Bake in oven for 25 minutes at 350 degrees. Serves four.

NOTES

Some nutmeg and cherry brandy would make this even better!

Potsta Sauce

INGREDIENTS

- 6 ounces Tomato Paste
- 2 tablespoons Olive Oil
- 1/2 cup Onions, Chopped
- 1/2 cup cannabis, Powdered
- 1 pinch Pepper
- 6 ounces Water
- 1/2 Garlic, Minced
- 1 Bay Leaf
- 1 pinch Thyme
- 1/2 teaspoon Salt
- 1 teaspoon Italian Seasoning

- 1 teaspoon Oregano

DIRECTIONS

In a large pot over high heat, add olive oil and onions. When onions become translucent, add garlic, salt, pepper, and cannabis. Stir until garlic becomes translucent. Pour water into pot, along with the bay leaf, thyme, Italian seasoning, and oregano. Once combined, add tomato paste. When mixture starts to bubble, reduce heat to medium-low and simmer for at least 2 hours.

NOTES

Substitute olive oil with Cannabis Cooking Oil. Meat lovers can brown 1 pound of ground beef and add it into the sauce to simmer.

Banana Bud Bread

INGREDIENTS

- 1/2 cup Shortening
- 2 Eggs
- 1 teaspoon Lemon Juice
- 3 teaspoons Baking Powder
- 1 cup Sugar
- 1 cup Mashed Bananas
- 2 cups Sifted Flour
- 1/2 cup cannabis, Powdered
- 1/2 teaspoon Salt
- 1 cup Nuts, Chopped

DIRECTIONS

Mix the shortening, sugar, and eggs together. Separately mix bananas with lemon juice and add to first mixture. Sift flour, salt, and baking powder together, and then mix all the ingredients together. Bake for 1 hour and 15 minutes at 375 degrees.

NOTES

For the best tasting banana bread, use bananas that have the "bruised" spots all over them. In addition, you can substitute with Cannashortening instead of adding straight cannabis.

Chocolate Peanut Butter Ganja Cookies

INGREDIENTS

- 1 cup flour
- 1/2 tsp baking soda
- 1/2 tsp salt
- 1/2 cup butter
- 1 1/2 cup brown sugar
- 1 tsp vanilla extract
- 1 egg
- 1 cup crunchy peanut butter
- 8 oz semisweet chocolate

DIRECTIONS

1. Sift together flour, baking soda, and salt -- set aside.
2. Melt butter and combine with sugar.
3. Add egg and vanilla to sugar/butter combination.
4. Add peanut butter to wet mixture.
5. Melt chocolate and add to wet mixture.
6. Gradually add dry ingredients.
7. Refrigerate until dough is firm and easy to work with.

8. Form one-inch balls, place on greased cookie sheet.

9. Flatten into cookies using the back of a fork (to form a cross hatch pattern).

10. Bake in a 350-degree oven approximately 10 minutes.

<u>Ganja Cinnamon Bread</u>

INGREDIENTS

- 1 cup white sugar
- 2 teaspoons baking powder
- 1/2 teaspoon baking soda
- 1 1/2 teaspoons ground cinnamon
- 1 cup buttermilk
- 1/4 cup vegetable oil
- 2 eggs
- 2 teaspoons vanilla extract
- 2 tablespoons white sugar
- 2 cups all-purpose flour
- 1 teaspoon salt
- 1 teaspoon ground cinnamon
- 2 teaspoons margarine/4 teaspoons cannabutter or as much marijuana as you need

DIRECTIONS

Preheat oven to 350 degrees F (175 degrees C). Grease one 9x5 inch loaf pan. Measure flour, 1 cup sugar, baking powder, baking soda, 1 1/2 teaspoons cinnamon, salt, buttermilk, oil, eggs and vanilla into large mixing bowl. Beat 3 minutes. Pour into prepared loaf pan. Smooth top. Combine 2 tablespoons white sugar, 1 teaspoon cinnamon and butter, mixing until crumbly. Sprinkle topping over smoothed batter. Using knife, cut in a light swirling motion to give a marbled effect.

Bake for about 50 minutes. Test with toothpick. When inserted it should come out clean. Remove bread from pan to rack to cool.

Leary Biscuit

INGREDIENTS

- 1 Ritz Cracker
- 1 teaspoon Butter
- 1/2 slice Cheese
- 1 gram cannabis

DIRECTIONS

Take a Ritz cracker, smear it with butter, add some cheese, and put the cannabis on top. Microwave on high for 35-40 seconds, or until the cheese is melted.

NOTES

You do not need to "activate" the THC in cannabis.

Tomahawk Ribeye

Cooking Time: 15 minutes

Servings: 4

Ingredients:

Directions:

1. Put a cast-iron pan in an oven and preheat it to almost 500°F.

2. Rub steaks with canola oil and sprinkle pepper and salt as per taste. Carefully remove hot skillet from oven, but wear oven mitt before touching skillet. Put this skillet on the stove over a high flame. Place marinated steak on this skillet and sear for almost one minute. Turn the side of steak and sear it again for one minute. Flip this steak again and put this skillet carefully to the oven. Cook in the oven for almost 3 minutes and flip the side of steak. Cook for another 3 minutes or until the thermometer shows 140°F.

3. Remove this steak from oven and tent this steak with an aluminum foil for almost ten minutes. Separate meat from its bone and cut thick slices. Top with delicious cannabutter and serve.

Healthy Cranberry Bars

Serving: 36

Prep Time: 20 minutes

Cook Time: 40 minutes

Ingredients

Crust

- ¼ teaspoon salt
- 1 and ½ teaspoon vanilla
- ¾ cup sugar
- ¾ cup cold Cannabutter
- ¾ cup brown sugar packed firmly into cup
- 1 and ½ cups flour
- 3 beaten eggs

Topping

- 2 cups sweetened flaked coconut
- 1 cup sweetened dried cranberries

How To:

1. Pre-heat your oven to 350 degrees F
2. Take a bowl and mix in flour and sugar
3. Add Cannabutter to the flour mixture and transfer to food processor, process until you have a coarse and crumbly mixture
4. Take the mixture and press it along 9x13 inch baking pan
5. Bake until golden
6. Take a bowl and mix in all the topping ingredients and mix well
7. Take the topping mix and pour over crust
8. Spread evenly, bake for 20-25 minutes until golden
9. Let the bars cool
10. Let it cool
11. Slice and serve
12. Enjoy!

Popcorn

INGREDIENTS

- 3 tablespoons Vegetable Oil
- 1/2 cup Popping Corn
- 1/8 ounce cannabis

DIRECTIONS

1. Put the oil in a tall pot, like the ones used for boiling spaghetti, and combine with finely chopped cannabis. Stir over medium-low heat

2. until the oil turns green in color. Put 1-2 kernels in the oil and when they begin to pop, add the rest of the corn. Cover the pot, and shake during popping until the popping noise dies down. Remove the pot from heat. The corn will finish popping. Remove lid and add butter and salt.

NOTES

You can always use microwave popcorn, but you'll have to use Cannabutter as a topping. Top your finished popcorn with Cannabutter to give it an extra punch.

Extra Green Avacado Dip

INGREDIENTS

- 3 ripe Avocados
- 1/2 cup chopped Onions
- 2 tsp Chilli Powder
- 3 tbs Wine Vinegar
- 1/2 cup finely chopped Marijuana

DIRECTIONS

Mix the vinegar, marijuana, and chilli powder together and let the mixture stand for one hour. Then add avocados and onions and mash it all together. It can be served with tacos or as a dip.

Delicious Tilapia

Cooking Time: 45 minutes

Servings: 4

Directions:

1. Preheat your oven to 375°F. Grease a baking pan with cooking spray.

2. Rinse fillets with cold water and pat dry with your paper towels. Put these fillets in a greased baking dish and pour fresh lemon juice over fillets. Sprinkle pepper, parsley and garlic on these fillets.

3. Bake them in a preheated oven for almost 30 minutes. Remove fillets from oven and drizzle cannabutter over them. Keep them in oven for extra two minutes. Remove from oven and serve with your favorite sauce.

Deep Fried Bourbon Apples

Serving: 4

Prep Time: 10 minutes

Cook Time: 10-15 minutes

Ingredients

- 2 large apples, chopped and cored
- 2 tablespoons water
- 1 tablespoon bourbon
- ½ teaspoon lemon juice
- 1 tablespoon raisins
- 1 tablespoon Cannabutter
- 2 tablespoons packed brown sugar
- 1 teaspoon cinnamon

How To:

1. Add Cannabutter, bourbon, water in a large sized skillet and place it over

1. medium heat

2. Stir well until butter melts

3. Add apples, brown sugar, cinnamon and raisins

4. Stir well to coat, bring the mix to a boil

5. Lower down heat and let it simmer

6. Once the apples are tender, stir in lemon juice and let it simmer for 10 minutes more

7. Serve and enjoy!

Devils On Horseback

Cooking Time: 20 minutes

Servings: 8

Ingredients:

Directions:

1. Preheat your oven to almost 325°F.

2. Use a knife to slit dates and spread them on a tray. Keep them aside.

3. Take a bowl and mix cannabutter and goat cheese. Equally fill this mixture in the dates and press into the middle and close dates after filling them.

4. Wrap one slice of bacon around stuffed date and replicate this process with all dates. Put these dates (seam down bacon) on your baking sheet.

5. Bake until the bacon turns crispy and it will take almost ten minutes.

Authentic CBD Infused Gingerbread

Serving: 10-12

Prep Time: 10 minutes

Cook Time: 35 minutes

Ingredients

- 1 cup flour

- 1 whole egg

- ½ teaspoon baking powder

- ½ teaspoon salt

- ½ teaspoon cinnamon

- ¼ teaspoon baking soda

- ½ teaspoon ginger, ground

- ¼ teaspoon ground cloves

- ½ cup water

- ½ cup molasses

- ½ cup Cannabutter

- ¼ cup sugar

- ¼ cup shortening

How To:

1. Pre-heat your oven to 350 degrees F

2. Take a bowl and add baking soda, flour, baking powder, salt, spices

3. Mix in water and molasses and mix well

4. Take a bowl and add shortening and beat until creamy

5. Slowly add sugar, egg and keep mixing until fluffy

6. Slowly add flour mixture and beat well

7. Pour the whole batter into an 8 inch greased pan and transfer to your oven

8. Bake for 35 minutes

9. Let it cool and serve

10. Enjoy!

Mama Budz Pesto

INGREDIENTS

- 1/2 cup Basil, chopped
- 1/2 cup fresh cannabis
- 1 cup Olive Oil
- 1/2 cup Parmesan, Grated
- 1/2 cup Romano, Grated
- Garlic

DIRECTIONS

Mix all ingredients in a food processor and refrigerate for at least 24 hours. Simple and delicious!

NOTES

Make sure you use fresh herbs, very important! Add pesto to your spaghetti or anything else you can think of.

Cannabaklava

INGREDIENTS

- 1 1/2 pounds Walnuts, Chopped
- 2 cups Sugar
- 1/2 teaspoon Nutmeg
- 3 teaspoons Cinnamon
- 3 sticks Butter
- 1/2 ounce cannabis, Powdered
- 16 ounces Filo Dough
- 1 1/2 cup Water

- 1 1/2 teaspoon Lemon Juice
- 2 cups Honey
- 1/2 teaspoon Vanilla

DIRECTIONS

Prepare the Cannabutter using all but 2 tablespoons of butter. Grease a 10x15inch baking dish with remaining butter. Lay 10 layers of filo dough down, coating each layer with liberal amounts of butter. You should have 1/3 of your butter left after doing this. The filo dough will be too big for the pan. Do not grease the sides, as you will want to cut off the excess filo dough so the dough just curves up slightly against the sides. Mix walnuts and 1-cup sugar. Pour into pan and spread evenly. Cut 5 more sheets of dough, just slightly bigger than the pan and repeat the same process in as before with the filo dough. Preheat the oven to 300 degrees, and bake for 50 minutes. During the baking process, mix the remaining sugar with water, lemon, vanilla, and spices. Cook in a saucepan until it is syrup, add honey and heat for another minute. When the baklava is done cooking, cut into 2x2-inch squares, and pour the honey-lemon sauce over the baklava. Let sit for 48 hours until the honey permeates everything.

NOTES

If all else fails, call your preacher.

<u>Key-F Lime Pie</u>

INGREDIENTS

- 1/4 cup Water
- 1 package Gelatin, Unflavored
- 1 cup Sugar
- 1/2 teaspoon Salt
- 4 Eggs, Separated
- 1/2 cup Lime Juice
- 3 teaspoons Lime Zest
- 1 cup Whipping Cream
- 1/2 cup Pistachio Nuts, Shelled, Unsalted
- Sweetened Whipping Cream
- Lime Slices
- Pastry Crust:
- 1/4 cup Cannabutter, Softened
- 1 cup Pastry Flour, Whole
- Wheat
- 1 large Egg Yolk
- Pinch of Salt
- 1/4 cup Raw Sugar

DIRECTIONS

Combine water and gelatin. Allow to soften for 5 minutes. Mix in salt, egg yolks, juice of lime, and half the sugar. Stir constantly over medium heat, just until boiling. Remove pan from heat, stir in 2 teaspoons of lime zest. Pour the mixture into a bowl and chill until slightly jelled. Gradually add the remaining sugar to the cream, and whip until stiff peaks form. Fold into the chilled, somewhat jelled mixture. Fill the pastry crust (directions follow) and chill the pie until the filling has set. Spread more sweetened whipped cream over the pie, place the slices of fresh lime around the edge, and sprinkle the center with the pistachios and remaining lime zest. Pastry crust: Blend the butter with the flour until you have a grainy mixture. Blend the egg, yolks, salt, and sugar together, and beat into the flour-butter mixture. Cover and refrigerate for 2 hours. Work the dough into your pie pan with lightly buttered fingers. Poke holes in the bottom and sides with a fork, to let steam out during cooking. Bake in a 400degree oven for 20 minutes.

NOTES

This recipe makes one 10-inch crust, with about one dose per teaspoon per slice. To cut potency, use half Cannabutter and half regular butter.

Mary "Vanilla Crisps" Jane

INGREDIENTS

- 1 Egg
- 2 cups Sugar
- 2 teaspoons Vanilla Extract
- 1 cup Cannabutter, Softened

DIRECTIONS

Mix the egg, sugar, vanilla, and Cannabutter in a large bowl until creamy in texture. Add the flour, making sure to incorporate the entire mixture. Cover the bowl, and refrigerate for 1 hour. Preheat oven to 375 degrees. With a #20 ice cream scooper, form the dough into balls and place on an ungreased cookie sheet. Leave about 2 inches between the balls. Take a glass out with a nice diameter, and wet the bottom and dip it in some sugar to coat the bottom. Press the cookies down with the bottom of the glass, but not too flat. Cook 8-10 minutes, or until golden brown.

NOTES

Doesn't really mask the taste of cannabis, but it's good if you like vanilla.

Stir Fry Vegan

Cooking Time: 25 minutes

Servings: 3 to 4

Ingredients:

Directions:

1. Steam the cubes of pumpkin for almost four minutes and keep aside.

2. Take a frying pan and heat oil. Add tofu and eggplant in this oil and let them fry to make crispy. Now add ginger-garlic paste and mix them to combine. Add soy sauce to this mixture along beans and pepper. Stir fry until you get crunchy ingredients. Add steamed pumpkin and mix them well to combine. Turn off heat, squeeze half lemon and sprinkle coriander. Garnish with lime wedges and serve with hot sauce, wild rice or quinoa.

Baked Potatoes with Cannabis

Cooking Time: 2 hours

Servings: 6

Ingredients:

Optional:

Directions:

1. Preheat an oven to almost 375 degrees F.

2. Put potatoes on one baking sheet and bake them for nearly an hour. Remove potatoes from oven and let the potatoes cool. Cut off each potato lengthwise. Scoop out the inner part of potato to get a bowl like shape. Be careful while scooping potato so that the skin should securely hold the shape of a potato. Mix the scooped out potatoes, cannabutter, and sour cream. Sprinkle pepper and salt. Mix all these ingredients together to get a smooth paste. Stuff the mixture of potato in the hollow skins of potatoes and bake for almost 10 minutes or let the top turn light brown. Top with butter and enjoy.

Sensual Chocolate Strawberries

Serving: 4

Prep Time: 10 minutes

Cook Time: 10 minutes

Ingredients

- 8 strawberries
- 1 cup dark chocolate chips
- 2 tablespoons Cannabutter

How To:

1. Make your double boiler over the stove and melt the dark chocolate chips and Cannabutter over medium-low heat

2. Whisk well while it is melting

3. Dry strawberries and dip them in melted chocolate

4. Transfer to waxed paper and let it dry

5. Let it cool and serve

6. Enjoy!

Twig Tea

INGREDIENTS

- 1-2 cups cannabis Stems
- 2 cups Water

DIRECTIONS

Grind your stems into a powder using either a hand grinder, coffee grinder, or mortar and pestle. In a saucepan, bring water to a rolling boil. Add the ground up stems, cover, and reduce heat to low. Let steep for 5-10 minutes, and then toss in a teabag or two of your favorite tea. Let steep another 5 minutes. Serve from a teapot that has a strainer in the spout, or strain your tea using a tea strainer, cheesecloth, or coffee filter.

NOTES

You could always add some honey or sugar to add more flavor.

Triple Chocolate S'Moores Marijuana Pie

INGREDIENTS

- 1 1/4 cups Graham Cracker Crumbs
- 1/4 cup Sugar

- 1/3 cup Cannabutter, Melted
- 1 cup Milk Chocolate Chips
- 1 cup White Chocolate Chips
- 1 cup Dark Chocolate Chips
- 1 1/2 cups Sweetened Condensed Milk
- 1 1/2 teaspoons Vanilla Extract
- 1 1/2 cups Miniature Marshmallows

DIRECTIONS

1. Preheat oven to 375 degrees. Spray inside of a 9-inch pie pan with non-stick cooking spray. In a bowl, combine graham cracker crumbs, sugar, and melted Cannabutter. Press mixture firmly into sprayed pie pan, covering bottom and sides. Blind bake (to bake without any filling) for 6-8 minutes, set aside to cool. For the filling, combine milk chocolate chips, 1/2 cup condensed milk, and 1/2 teaspoon vanilla. Stir until chips are melted then pour into bottom of cooled crust. Set in refrigerator while preparing the second layer. Repeat the above process using the white chocolate chips, and again with the dark chocolate chips. Make sure to let set in refrigerator between each layer. Preheat the broiler. Open a bag of miniature marshmallows. Remove pie from refrigerator and cover evenly with miniature marshmallows. Place under broiler for 1-2 minutes until marshmallows begin to brown. Refrigerate at least 1 hour before serving.

NOTES

You could always use a torch to brown the marshmallows; I find it's a little easier to get an even brown compared to using the broiler.

Sassy Chocolate Covered Grapes

Serving: 4

Prep Time: 20-30 minutes

Cook Time: 10 minutes

Ingredients

- 4 cups grapes
- ½ cup Cannabutter
- 1 pound milk chocolate

How To:

1. Prepare your double-boiler over the stove top and set the temperature to medium-low heat
2. Add Cannabutter and melt it, keep it on the side
3. Add chocolate to your double boiler and melt the chocolate as well
4. Re-introduce the melted Cannabutter to the pan with melted chocolate
5. Mix well until incorporated well
6. Take your grapes and dry them well
7. Dip in chocolate mixture and transfer them to waxed paper
8. Let the chocolate harden and let it cool
9. Serve and enjoy!

<u>Peanut Butter – Butter Bars</u>

Serving: 12

Prep Time: 25 minutes

Cook Time: 15 minutes

Ingredients

- 4 tablespoons peanut butter

- 1 cup melted Cannabutter

- 1 cup peanut butter

- 1 and ½ cups semisweet chocolate chips

- 2 cups Graham cracker crumbs

- 2 cups confectioner's sugar

How To:

1. Add Cannabutter, confectioners' sugar, graham cracker crumbs, peanut butter to a medium-sized bowl

2. Stir well until firm and transfer the mix to a 9 x 13-inch baking pan, press

1. until firm

2. Transfer your chocolate to a microwave oven bowl and melt it, add peanut butter and mix well to form the peanut butter mix

3. Make sure to keep stirring it from time to time

4. Transfer the mixture to your cooled crust and let it chill

5. Cut into squares and serve

6. Enjoy!

Amazing CBD Chocolate Cup-Cakes

Serving: 12

Prep Time: 10-20 minutes

Cook Time: 15-25 minutes

Ingredients

- 1 box premade cake mix
- 1/3 cup Cannabutter, melted
- ¼ cup milk
- 3 whole eggs
- 1 container frosting
- 1 cup chocolate chips

How To:

1. Pre-heat your oven to 325 degrees F
2. Take a large bowl and add the cake mix
3. Add eggs, milk, and Cannabutter
4. Beat well until lightly moist
5. Mix on medium speed using a hand blender for about 2 minutes until the mixture is blended well
6. Add chocolate chips to the mixture
7. Take your cupcake tray and line it with cupcake liners
8. Fill them up about 2/3rds of the way
9. Transfer to your oven

10. Bake for 15-20 minutes until a toothpick comes out clean from the center

11. Once done, remove from oven and let it cool for 20 minutes

12. Spread icing and serve

13. Enjoy!

Simple Canna Banana Muffins

Serving: 12

Prep Time: 15 minutes

Cook Time: 15 minutes

Ingredients

- 1 and ½ cups self-rising flour
- ½ cup brown sugar
- ½ teaspoon baking soda
- ½ cup banana, mashed
- ½ cup Cannaoil (cannabis infused oil)
- 1 whole egg, whisked
- ¾ cup milk
- ½ cup light cream cheese

How To:

1. Pre-heat your oven to 350 degrees F
2. Take your muffin tray and grease it well
3. Take a large bowl and add flour, baking soda, sugar and mix well until incorporated
4. Make a well in the center
5. Take another bowl and add mashed banana, egg, oil, and milk

6. Pour the mixture into the well and stir gently until thoroughly combined

7. Spoon the mixture evenly into your greased muffin tray

8. Bake for 15 minutes until a toothpick comes out clean from the center

9. Remove from oven and let it cool

10. Serve with ice cream and enjoy!

Jalapeno Ganja Muffins

INGREDIENTS

- 1/2 cup Cannabutter
- 1/3 cup Raw Sugar
- 2 large Eggs
- 8 ounces Creamed Corn
- 1 cup Sour Cream
- 1/2 teaspoon Sea Salt
- 1 tablespoon Aluminum-Free Baking Powder
- 1/2 cup All-Purpose Flour, Unbleached
- 1 cup Sharp Cheddar Cheese, Grated
- 1/4 cup Lemon Zest
- 1/2 cup Jalapeno Peppers, Chopped, Seeded
- 1 1/2 cups Yellow Corn Meal

DIRECTIONS

In a large bowl, cream together the butter, sugar, eggs, creamed corn, and sour cream. Sift the salt, baking powder, and flour, and then combine with the creamed mixture. Stir in the grated cheese, lemon zest, peppers, and corn mea. If necessary, adjust the taste with a little bit of sugar at a time. Grease muffin tins with

Cannabutter, and fill the cups 2/3 full. Bake in preheated 450-degree oven for 18-20 minutes.

NOTES

If you want it really spicy, like me, try some other peppers or mix in some horseradish with the sour cream.

Creative Canna Blueberry Muffins

Serving: 12

Prep Time: 15 minutes

Cook Time: 20 minutes

Ingredients

For Cupcake

- ½ teaspoon salt
- 2 teaspoon baking powder
- 1/3 cup sugar
- ½ cup Cannabutter
- 1 cup milk
- 2 cups flour
- 1 eggs, slightly beaten
- 1 cup fresh/frozen blueberries
- Icing
- 1/4 cup melted butter
- ¼ cup sugar

How To:

1. Pre-heat your oven to 35 degrees F
2. Position your rack in the center of the oven

3. Grease muffin tin with paper liners

4. Take a large bowl and beat in Cannabutter, sugar with electric mixer until fluffy

5. Add egg, one at a time and keep beating it after every addition

6. Add remaining ingredients, making sure to add blueberries last

7. Pour the mixture into muffin trays and bake for 20-25 minutes, until a toothpick comes out clean from the center

8. Take them out and let them sit for 10 minutes

9. Prepare the icing by mixing the icing ingredients and spread the mixture over the warm muffins

10. Serve and enjoy!

The Basic Cannabis Muffins

Serving: 12

Prep Time: 10 minutes

Cook Time: 25 minutes

Ingredients

- ¼ cup Cannabutter
- 2 cups all-purpose flour
- ½ teaspoon salt
- 3 teaspoons baking powder
- ¾ cup white sugar
- 1 whole egg
- 1 cup milk

How To:

1. Pre-heat your oven to 350 degrees F

2. Take a saucepan and melt your Cannabutter over low heat

3. Keep it on the side

4. Take a large bowl and stir in baking powder, flour, sugar, and salt

5. Mix well

6. Make a well in the center

7. Take a small bowl and beat in eggs, stir in milk and Cannabutter

8. Pour the whole mixture into the well and quickly mix until moist

9. Pour the lumpy batter into your muffin cups

10. Bake for 25 minutes until golden

11. Serve and enjoy!

Raunchy Cinnamon Mini Cupcakes

Serving: 24

Prep Time: 15 minutes

Cook Time: 15 minutes

Ingredients

- 1 and ¼ teaspoon baking powder
- ¼ cup Cannabutter, melted
- 1/3 cup white sugar + ¼ cup white sugar
- ½ cup milk
- 1 cup all-purpose flour
- 1 beaten egg
- 1 tablespoon cinnamon
- Filling such as strawberry, raspberry, etc.

How To:

1. Pre-heat your oven to 375 degrees F
2. Take a large sized bowl and sift in baking powder, flour, sugar
3. Whisk in Cannabutter, milk, egg to a bowl
4. Add the dry mixture into the liquid mixture and mix well
5. Pour the mixture into muffin pans and bake for 10-12 minutes
6. Take a bowl and add ¼ cup white sugar, cinnamon
7. Once the muffins are done, take them out and coat with more melted Cannabutter and the cinnamon and sugar mix
8. Add your desired jam on top and enjoy!

Honey And Banana Muffins

Serving: 12

Prep Time: 15 minutes

Cook Time: 20-25 minutes

Ingredients

*   ½ teaspoon baking soda
*   ½ teaspoon salt
*   1 teaspoon baking powder
*   2 tablespoons honey
*   ¼ cup Cannabutter, melted
*   2/3 cup milk
*   1 cup bran cereal
*   2 eggs, beaten
*   1/3 cup firmly packed brown sugar

- 1 cup ripe bananas, mashed
- 1 and ½ cups flour

How To:

1. Pre-heat your oven to 375 degrees F
2. Place oven rack in center of the oven
3. Take a muffin tin and grease it/ line with muffin liners
4. Take a bowl and add bran cereal and milk, let it sit for 5 minutes
5. Take another bowl and add bananas, brown sugar, Cannabutter, honey, eggs and mix well
6. Add the dry ingredients (baking powder, salt, baking soda, and flour) to the mixture and stir well
7. Pour the batter into your muffin tins
8. Bake for 20-25 minutes until a toothpick comes out clean from center
9. Serve and enjoy!

Spicy Carrot Cupcakes With Creamy Frosting

Serving: 12

Prep Time: 20 minutes

Cook Time: 20 minutes

Ingredients

For Cupcake

- 1 and ½ cups all-purpose flour
- 1 teaspoon baking soda
- ½ teaspoon ground cinnamon
- ½ teaspoon ground allspice

- ¼ teaspoon nutmeg
- ¼ teaspoon salt
- 2 large whole eggs
- 1 and ¼ cups brown sugar
- ¼ cup Cannabutter, melted
- ¼ cup orange juice
- ½ teaspoon vanilla extract
- ½ cup raisins
- ¼ cup walnuts, chopped
- 1 and ½ cups shredded carrot

Frosting

- Shredded coconut
- 8 ounces cream cheese
- ¾ cup confectioner's sugar
- ½ teaspoon vanilla extract

How To:

1. Pre-heat your oven to 350 degrees F
2. Prepare your muffin tray by placing muffin cups
3. Take a medium bowl and whisk in flour, baking soda, salt and spices
4. Take a large bowl and beat in sugar, eggs until smooth
5. Whisk in melted Cannabutter, orange juice, and vanilla extract
6. Stir in flour mixture into the liquid mix
7. Stir in shredded carrots and divide the mixture onto your muffin pans
8. Bake for 16-18 minutes until a toothpick comes out clean from the center

9. Remove from oven and let it cool

10. Take a medium bowl and add the frosting ingredients, whisk them well

11. Spread the frosting over your cooled cupcakes and top with coconut

12. Enjoy!

Subtle Vanilla Macaroon Cupcakes

Serving: 48

Prep Time: 35 minutes

Cook Time: 15-17 minutes

Ingredients

For Cupcake

- 1 teaspoon vanilla
- ¼ cup milk
- 3 ounces soft cream cheese
- ¾ cup soft butter
- 1 cup sweetened flaked coconut
- 1 and ½ cups flour
- 1 and ¾ cups sugar
- 3 whole eggs

Frosting

- 3-4 tablespoons whip cream
- 1/3 cup soft Cannabutter
- 4 ounces melted white chocolate
- ¾ cup sweetened flaked coconut
- 3 cups powdered sugar

How To:

1. Pre-heat your oven to 350 degrees F

2. Take your cupcake tray and line it with muffin liners

3. Take a big bowl and mix in butter, cream cheese, sugar and beat until creamy

4. Once the mixture has been beaten, add remaining ingredients and mix well

5. Pour batter into cupcake liners and bake for 15-17 minutes

6. Take them out and let them cool for a while

7. Prepare the frosting by mixing all the frosting ingredients and spread the mixture over warm cupcakes

8. Serve and enjoy!

Delicious Black Forest Muffins

Serving: 20

Prep Time: 15 minutes

Cook Time: 20 minutes

Ingredients

For Cupcake

- ½ teaspoon baking soda
- ½ cup Cannabutter
- ½ cup roughly cut dark chocolate
- ¾ cup brown sugar
- ¼ cup cocoa powder
- ¾ cup milk
- 1 and ¼ cups self-rising flour
- 2 whole eggs

- 15 ounces dark cherries
- 1 tablespoon cocoa
- 1 teaspoon icing sugar

How To:

1. Pre-heat your oven to 350 degrees F
2. Prepare your muffin tray with muffin liners
3. Take a bowl and add butter and sugar, add eggs one at a time and keep mixing
4. Take a bowl and add baking soda, flour, and cocoa
5. Sift the mixture and transfer to the butter and egg mix
6. Add milk, chocolate, and cherries to the batter and mix
7. Once the batter is ready, pour the mixture into your cupcake tins, fill each hole to about ¾
8. Bake for 20-25 minutes until a toothpick comes out clean
9. Once done, frost it well and enjoy!

CHAPTER 8
OTHER SWEET TREATS

Amazing CBD Infused Berry Parfait

Serving: 4

Prep Time: 10 minutes

Cook Time: 5-10 minutes

Ingredients

- 3 cups plain yogurt
- 2 cups raspberries
- 2 cups blackberries
- ½ cup granola
- ½ cup sugar
- ¼ cup honey
- 1 tablespoon vanilla extract
- 1/3 cup orange liqueur
- ¾ cup CBD infused-coconut oil

How To:

1. Take a bowl and mix in coconut oil and yogurt
2. Add orange liqueur, honey and vanilla extract to the pan
3. Place it over medium-low heat
4. Once the mixture is slightly hot, add blackberries and reduce them
5. The whole mixture should turn into a nice compote
6. Remove from heat

7. Take a tall glass and fill it with 2 spoonfuls of yogurt, 6 raspberries, a spoonful of compote and sprinkle of granola

8. Repeat until all the mixture has been used up

9. Serve and enjoy!

Exquisite Chocolaty- Banana Sundae

Serving: 4

Prep Time: 10 minutes

Cook Time: 5-10 minutes

Ingredients

For Canna Chocolate Sauce

- 8 ounces dark chocolate, finely chopped
- 1 cup heavy cream
- 2 tablespoons Cannabutter

For Sunday

- 2 scoops vanilla ice cream
- ¼ cup chocolate sauce
- 1 banana
- Whipped cream
- Your desired amount of nuts for sprinkling

How To:

1. Create a double-boiler over medium heat and add Cannabutter with cream, let it heat up

2. Once the butter has melted, stir in chocolate and wait until incorporated

3. Allow the sauce to cool for 5 minutes

4. Cut banana in half

5. Take your ice cream dish and arrange everything according to your mood!

6. Drizzle ¼ cup chocolate sauce on top and enjoy!

The Big Awesome Apple Pie

Serving: 8

Prep Time: 30 minutes

Cook Time: 60 minutes

Ingredients

- 2 cups all-purpose flour
- ½ teaspoon salt
- ½ cup Cannabutter
- ½ cup ice water
- 8 Granny Smith Apples, peeled, cored and sliced
- 1 cup white sugar
- 1 tablespoon extra all-purpose flour
- 1 and ½ teaspoons ground cinnamon
- 2 tablespoons extra Cannabutter

How To:

1. Take a large bowl and add salt, flour, and Cannabutter

2. Mix well until you have a coarse mixture

3. Stir in a tablespoon of water and keep mixing until you have a nice ball

4. Divide the dough in half and shape the balls

5. Wrap them in plastic and let them chill for 4 hours/overnight

6. Roll one ball out to a 9-inch pie plate

7. Place bottom crust in your pie plate

8. Roll out top crust and keep it on the side

9. Pre-heat your oven to 400 degrees F

10. Take a large bowl and add sliced apples, 1 tablespoon flour, sugar, cinnamon

11. Mix well and pour the mixture into your pie shell

12. Dot with remaining 2 tablespoons butter

13. Cover with top crust

14. Seal the edges and cut any extra side dough

15. Make slits on top

16. Bake for 60 minutes

17. Serve and enjoy!

Heartwarming Chocolate Pudding

Serving: 10

Prep Time: 10 minutes

Cook Time: 10minutes

Ingredients

- 2 cups whole milk
- 2 egg whites
- ½ cup sugar
- 2 tablespoons cornstarch
- 10 tablespoons unsweetened cocoa
- 3 tablespoons melted Cannabutter
- 1 teaspoon vanilla extract
- Raspberries (optional)

How To:

1. Take a bowl and lightly beat the eggs, keep on the side

2. Take a medium bowl and add cornstarch, cocoa, and mix

3. Whisk in 1 cup milk and whisk again

4. Add remaining milk, butter, and sugar in a pan over medium heat and bring it to a gentle boil

5. Whisk the mixture well and lower down the heat, simmer for 2 minutes

6. Add cocoa mix after the simmer

7. Increase heat to medium and bring to boil, lower down to simmer, make sure to keep whisking the mixture throughout the whole process

8. Remove heat and let it cool for 10 minutes

9. Once cooled, add a cup of egg whites and whisk well

10. Return the whole mixture to heat and cook on low for a few minutes

11. Remove from heat

12. Add vanilla extract and let it cool

13. Once done, transfer to the fridge

14. Once chilled, sprinkle raspberries and serve

15. Enjoy!

Delicious Foster Banana

Serving: 1-2

Prep Time: 10 minutes

Cook Time: 5 minutes

Ingredients

- ½ cup Cannabutter
- 1 cup superfine sugar

- 4 bananas, peeled and halved lengthwise
- ½ cup coconut ice cream

How To:

1. Take a large heavy skillet and place it over medium heat
2. Add Cannabutter and let it melt
3. Stir in sugar and cook, stirring it gently until the sugar is lightly brown
4. Add bananas in the pan and cook for 2 minutes
5. Serve with coconut ice cream
6. Enjoy!

Fantastic Sriracha Fudgesicles

Serving: 8

Prep Time: 10 minutes

Cook Time: 5-10 minutes

Ingredients

- 1/3 cup sugar
- 1 tablespoon cornstarch
- 2 tablespoons semisweet chocolate chips
- 1 and ¼ cup Cannamilk
- 2 tablespoons unsweetened cocoa powder
- 1 teaspoon Sriracha
- ½ tablespoons Cannabutter
- ½ teaspoon vanilla extract
- Pinch of salt
- Crushed peanuts, optional

How To:

1. Take a saucepan and place it over low heat
2. Add chocolate and let it melt
3. Stir in cocoa powder, cornstarch, milk, sugar, sriracha, salt
4. Mix well
5. Once incorporated well, increase heat to medium and gently stir for 5-10 minutes
6. Remove heat and add Cannabutter and vanilla
7. Stir well until combined
8. Keep it on the side and let it cool
9. Sprinkle peanuts into your popsicles and pour into molds
10. Insert sticks and let it freeze
11. Serve and enjoy!

THC Pills

INGREDIENTS

- 1/8th oz herb. (I used shwag the first time)
- 4oz Extra Virgin Olive Oil.
- 32 Empty Gelatin Pill Sleeves. (Get them online, or just go to the store and buy some cheap ginko biloba pills.)

DIRECTIONS

1. Put your herb in a blender for 2 minutes, till it is powder. Add a few tablespoons of water if it is super dry.
2. Move all herb into another container, use glass, it makes the process a lot easier. Then place in freezer overnight.
3. Remove from freezer, and in same container add your olive oil slowly! Add a little bit, then stir, a little bit more, stir, but stop when you have exceeded saturation point(when it starts to look more like a soup than a mixture).

4. Place in microwave for two minutes, covered.

5. Remove from microwave, stir vigorously, to help break up any particulates or clumps.

6. Place back into microwave for another minute.

7. Remove, you want it to be thick...almost like a tar. If it is still runny...zap it again. But DO NOT LET IT SMOKE! If it smokes, it's burning your WEED.

8. Stir, till it is even. It should at this point be a dark amber, but NOT black!

9. Line up your empty pills, inside your filler.

10. Take a spoonfull of your mix, then place it over the filler. Next use a playing card(clean) to evenly smear over your empty pill containers, so they are all evenly filled. Repeat till all pills are filled, then place tops on pills.

11. Repeat process till all THC mix is used.

12. Place pills in freezer for One day.(you can do this for just a few hours if you want.)

13. Clean up....that's it!

14. The fun begins! Just like cannabutter, you have to be weary of your tollerance. Heavy smokers report 2 pills of this from schwag kept them high for almost 10 hours.)

15. Take one pill your first time. It will take about an hour and a half to kick in. If you do not get your desired effect, take ONE more pill. But be sure not to drive anyplace. This will knock you on your ass.

16. Place pills back in freezer, or in the fridge. I like the fridge, because it doesn't take as long to digest.

17. That's it! They will keep for a long time. NOW HAVE SOME FUN!!! YOU WILL BE AS HIGH AS ALL HELL...BUT YOU WON'T HAVE COTTONMOUTH!

NOTES

For those of you whom do not have a pill filler, this is what you will have to do; take your tar mix, and add about 1oz oil. Place in microwave for 20 seconds. Mix, till smooth and workable. It should be about as thin as the oil was to begin with. Then use an eye dropped to place into your empty pills. Place caps on, and put it in the freezer. That's it. It's really simple!

Choco-Lovers Almond Bars

Serving: 24

Prep Time: 10 minutes

Cook Time: 10 minutes

Ingredients

- 1 cup crunchy almond butter
- 2 cups powdered sugar
- ½ cup Cannabutter, soft
- 1 tablespoon Cannabutter
- 1 and ½ cups Graham Cracker crumbs
- ¾ cup semisweet chocolate chips
- ¼ cup slivered almonds

How To:

1. Take a 9x13 inch pan and line it with foil
2. Take a medium saucepan and place it over medium heat
3. Add Cannabutter and let it melt, stir in powdered sugar, almond butter, and Graham Cracker Crumbs
4. Stir well until combined and press the mixture into your prepared pan

5. Take another small saucepan and place it over medium heat, add 1 tablespoon Cannabutter and add in chocolate chips, stir until melted

6. Spread almond mixture over your crumb mixture

7. Top with slivered almonds

8. Chill for 60 minutes and let it set

9. Cut into bars and enjoy!

NIPS

INGREDIENTS

- Saltine Crackers.

- Nutella (in the peanut butter aisle)

- Bowl of well broken up buds

DIRECTIONS

Put a mildly thick coat of nutella on two crackers (about 3 or 4 millimetres thick). Put .5 herb on the nutella spread onto one of the crackers. Put the crackers together like an oreo cookie. Put them on a cookie sheet and bake them at 325 degrees for 25 minutes.

NOTES

You can eat 2 cracker sandwiches. It takes about an hour to hit you

and can last for up to 6 hours so don't plan on driving anywhere!

Krispy Rice Squares

Serving: 10-12

Prep Time: 5 minutes

Cook Time: 5 minutes

Ingredients

- 2 tablespoons Cannabutter
- 2 cups mini-marshmallows
- 2 and ½ cups rice crispy cereal

How To:

1. Take a large sized saucepan and place it over low heat
2. Add Cannabutter and stir in marshmallows
3. Keep stirring the mixture for 2 minutes
4. Remove saucepan from heat and stir in cereal
5. Press the mixture into a buttered- wax paper lined 9x13 inch pan
6. Let it cool
7. Once cooled, slice into bars and serve
8. Enjoy

CONCLUSION

Cannabis is safe to use as medicinal drugs, and administered by a variety of methods, such as dried buds, vaporizing, eating cannabis, oral sprays, and capsules. Synthetic cannabinoids are useful for the treatment of nausea and vomiting. It is a reasonable treatment with lowest possible side-effects, such as orthostatic hypotension, ocular problem, pruritus, muscle twitching, hallucination and dry mouth. It is safe for the used treatment of HIV Aids and several neurological problems. Cannabis proved useful for the treatment of chronic pain, such as neuropathy and fibromyalgia.

There are a few intriguing pieces of evidence of medical cannabis to reduce posttraumatic stress disorders. It is essential to understand the pros and cons of the marijuana plant before using it. There are some particular applications for various diseases that will help you to use it in a right way. You should understand its drawbacks and contradictions with other drugs before using this plan. It is available in numerous forms, such as oils, powders, capsules, tablets and extracts. These are

useful for different diseases, and you should learn its proper use.